This work is dedicated to Jews,
Christians and Muslims.

CONTENTS

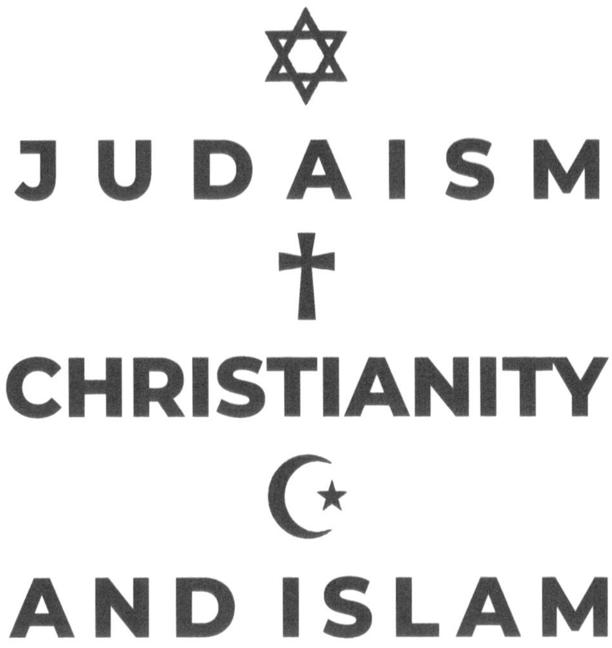

SIMILARITIES IN JUDAISM CHRISTIANITY AND ISLAM

HABILA T. DABOH

Foreword by Prof. Peter Bauna Tanko

www.virtualinsignia.com.ng

Published by
Virtual Insignia
1st Floor, Hamza Zayyad House,
4 Warf Road (Mohammed Buhari Way),
Kaduna, Nigeria

Mobile: +234 803 956 4442, +234 802 884 2372
e-mail: vitualinsignia@hotmail.com
website: www.virtualinsignia.com.ng

First Published, 2020

ISBN: 978-978-987-689-1

Imprimatur
Most Revd. Dr. Matthew Man-Oso Ndagoso
Catholic Archbishop of Kaduna

Printed in Nigeria by
Virtual Insignia Ltd.
Hamza Zayyad House,
4 Mohammed Buhari Way, Kaduna, Nigeria
www.virtualinsignia.com.ng

ACKNOWLEDGMENT

The year 2020 cannot easily be forgotten for so many reasons including the appalling experience of the COVID-19 pandemic. I thank God for keeping me alive to acknowledge His greatness and to write this book.

The writing of this book did not just happen. A number of persons encouraged me, especially my Archbishop, Matthew Man'oso Ndagoso. His dogged support made the writing of this book easier. My profound indebtedness is to Bishop Matthew Hassan Kukah who kept calling and encouraging me to stay calm and 'enjoy' the lockdown in Rome, as it was an occasion to read and write something.

I thank *Propaganda Fide* through Msgr. Hyacinthe Dione, *Direttore Collegio Missionario Internazionale san Giuseppe* in Rome where I lived while carrying out research for this book. I had more than enough light to work and their WI-FI never disappointed me. Many thanks to Srs. May and Gemma who looked after me and others. My words of appreciation are immeasurable to Rev. Fr. Prof. Joseph Mamman of Ahmadu Bello University Zaria who meticulously went through the manuscript and gave necessary suggestions in order to get rid of any theological misrepresentation in the work. Prof. Abdulkadir Aliyu Ladan of Ahmadu Bello University, Zaria, a Professor of Islam also took quality time to read the whole work to be sure it was free of Islamic blunder. Mr. Sarki Philip Ereson perused the work word after word to make it what it is. I thank them immensely. Rev. Fr. Prof. Peter Bauna Tanko graciously accepted to write the Forward to this book. In a few loaded paragraphs, he recapitulates the essence of the book. I thank him hugely. My gratitude is also due to friends and colleagues who assisted and supported me in many ways for the publication of this book.

FOREWORD

To describe this book as a *tour de force* would be an understatement. The author has beautifully woven in clear and simple language, key ideas bestriding the monotheistic religions of Judaism, Christianity and Islam. Through sound and critical analyses, the path to authentic perception of the three religions is illuminated paving the way towards sound dialogue.

This book is pastoral charity expressed in an extraordinary manner. Through this book adherents of the three religions are expected to cast off unnecessary prejudices that have led to loss of lives over religious superiority. Without distortion or bias, the author presents the concepts as each religion understands them, backing up his findings with credible sources. The reader can, therefore, follow the author from an intellectual, spiritual, and moral perspective, depending on his mood.

It is not so much what separates the three religions that is the issue. The distortion of the authentic teachings of these religions by few adherents for political gains leaves much to desire. This attitude creates unhealthy relationships among these religions and makes global peace illusive.

Unity of the human race lies in the fact that the entire human family has only one origin-God. Every human being bears in himself or herself something of the divine image of God and is created for the same final goal which is God Himself. Our differences are a less important element when confronted with a unity that is radical, fundamental and decisive. The author brings out this point in this book.

Academics and students of religion will find this book quite educative. Students, particularly in tertiary institutions, who study comparative religions and inter-religious dialogue will benefit a lot from this book. Realistic and incisive, this is essential reading for adherents of the monotheistic religions. I salute the author.

REV. FR. PROF. PETER BAUNA TANKO

Preface

Religion is a complex phenomenon with multifarious definitions. A definition that is inclusive of all the components of religion and distinguishes it from other relative concepts like magic, cults and sects, is not easily ascertained. Many people have suggested different definitions of religion without much knowledge of the wide range of religious trends and the many different cultural manifestations of the concept. To arrive at a near acceptable definition of religion would require understanding its etymology.

The most favoured origin of the word 'religion' is associated with the Roman grammarian, Servius (end of the 4th century A.D) supported by the view of the Christian Philosopher, Lactantius, through the ideas of the Roman philosophical poet, Lucretius. Lactantius (c.313A.D) quoted Lucretius' opinion that *religionum animum nodis exsolvere* (religious mind bonds fast)in proof that he considered the word 'ligare' --meaning to 'bind'--as the root of the word 'religion' (In institutions Divinae, 4, 28). This etymological understanding of religion has received a wider acclamation. Most secular and ecclesiastical dictionaries adopted 'ligare' as the root of religion.

However, modern dictionaries have departed from the word 'ligare' to describing religion and explaining it than taking off from it. According to the *Ecylopaedia Britannica*, **religion** is human beings' relation to that which they regard as holy, sacred, absolute, spiritual, divine, or worthy of special reverence. It is also now commonly regarded as consisting of the way people deal with ultimate concerns about their lives and their fate after death. For *dictionary.com*, religion is a set of beliefs concerning the cause, nature, and purpose of the universe, especially when considered as the creation of a superhuman agency or agencies, usually involving devotional and ritual observances, and often containing a moral code governing the conduct of human affairs.

Every religion has its own history of evolution, including the three Abrahamic religions which are the focus of this book. Although the Abrahamic religions are more than three, this book focuses on Judaism, Christianity and Islam, the most prevalent and popular religions on the planet earth.

Whatever form religion takes, it affects and influences human beings in different ways. History has shown that man accepts and accommodates religion as escape route against incomprehensible human situations. Those things that go beyond the intellectual capacity of the human mind are taken into spiritualism and categorised as mystery. Despite the scientific and technological expertise of the engineering world, there are issues that cannot be understood or explained away. At this point religion comes in.

Almost all religions are against negativism. When a certain religion does or practices something that is perceived wrong by others, it would have been positive by the adherents of that religion. Every religion preaches and encourages good attitude and behaviour. It is, therefore, not the religion that is bad but the devotees who depart from its good injunctions. Adherents of religion could be guilty of creating disharmony by opposing the beliefs of others because they feel and believe theirs is the 'right one'. When other religions are perceived to be 'others', or to be 'wrong' or their adherents perceived to be 'non believers', then the seed of discord is sown. Since every religion calls for love and appreciation of its members, this gesture should be extended across the board.

There is no doubt that religion has contributed positively to society. Religious beliefs, values and ideas have continued to make momentous involvement and contribute to the development of society. In sophisticated societies, religion and its meaningful belief systems articulate responses to issues relating to human nature, identity and purpose. In essence, these religions provide a frame of reference for understanding the world and for guiding personal and communal action for the good of all.

It is interesting to remind ourselves that some of the adherents of these religions who are supposed to be the moral guides of our societies have severally failed and plunged the same societies into chaos. Since Christianity, it is believed, more or less learnt from Judaism, and Islam from Christianity and Judaism, one would expect that these three Abrahamic religions, whose God is their Creator will appreciate each other and work together for the common good. However, it is surprising that the same God of Moses, Jesus and Muhammad will in one Holy book be merciful and compassionate, in another, order the killing of nonbelievers, and in another the God or war; or being all in every Holy Book. Could these seeming contradictions be from the founders of these religions or the adherents?

Jews, Christians and Muslims, it is believed, worship the same God. Yet, each believes that their religion contains the full and final revelation of the same God. Here, lies a manifestation of the origin of their unity and of their division. Since this belief in the truth of one religion and the falsity of the others leads to inevitable conflict between the believer and the unbeliever, the chosen and the rejected, the saved and the damned, here, again, lies the seed of intolerance and violence.

The ignorance and myopic view of religion by some people is the reason it is accused of causing many unpleasant happenings in the contemporary world. This is seen in the disagreements between different faith ideologies and creeds. Beyond disagreements, the trend extends to the killing of those who do not share the beliefs and practices of other religions in obedience to the command of their Holy Book. It is a given that some people believe in one religion and lose the competence to understand or to seek understanding and appreciate what others believe in. When this happens, people become both incredulous and suggestible leading to unimaginable ends.

In a multi-religious society, people should be at liberty to believe in any religion of their choice. However, it is not acceptable to think that one religion is above or beneath another in such kind of society. Beliefs, practices and values may differ; such differences should be respected for mutual understanding and coexistence.

The issues raised in this book would assist the reader to rediscover from the three Abrahamic religions, how different adherents to different religions have fared. It is intended to elucidate the mind of the reader to understand that as good as a religion could be, if not properly handled, it could be a source of discord. We shall see what roles these religions play in the lives of their members and the society. There are also the common practices and beliefs that these religions share. These common grounds should be respectfully maintained in honour of their source.

The perspective of lived faith is also anticipated by adherents of different religions. This way, the reader will identify and understand the worldviews and approaches to the teachings of every religion and the strict obedience to their foundations and traditions. The historical study of these religions would provide the reader the opportunity to develop an appreciation of the way the religion of other people contribute to multi-religious societies. At the end of reading this book, one should understand that these religions are meant to be good for all and not for individuals since the aim is to reunite with the creator on the Day of Judgment.

Solemnity of the
Immaculate Conception
Kaduna, 2020

CHAPTER ONE
THE ABRAHAMIC RELIGIONS

The Abrahamic religions, also referred to as Abrahamism, are a group of Semitic-originated religious communities of faith that claim descent from the practices of the ancient Israelites and the worship of the God of Abraham.[1] The term derives from a figure from the Bible known as Abraham. The major Abrahamic religions in chronological order of founding are Judaism in the 7th century BCE,[2] Christianity in the 1st century CE, and Islam in the 7th century CE. The Abrahamic religions are among the major divisions in comparative religion along with Indian, Iranian, and East Asian religions.[3]

Massignon (1949) opines that the phrase "Abrahamic religion" means all the religions that come from one spiritual source.[4] All the major Abrahamic religions claim a direct connection and ancestry to Abraham, although in Christianity this is understood in spiritual terms because Abraham is recorded in the Torah as the ancestor of the Israelites through his son Isaac, born by Sarah as found in Genesis 17: 16. The Jews believe that they are descendants of Abraham, and devotees of Judaism took their spiritual identity from Abraham as the first of the three biblical Patriarchs namely: Abraham, Isaac and Jacob. This is relevant to the words of Paul in Romans 4, where he refers to Abraham as the "father of us all".

---

[1] *"Philosophy of Religion".Encyclopedia Britannica. 2010.*

[2] *Atzmon, G.; Hao, L.; Pe'er, I.; et al. (June 2010).).*

[3] Adams, C.J. (2007). *Classification of religions: Geographical.* Encyclopedia Britannica.

[4] Massignon, L. (1949), pp. 20–23.

The Islamic tradition maintains that Muhammad, an Arab, descended from Abraham's son Ishmael. Jewish tradition also equates the descendants of Ishmael, (Ishmaelites), with Arabs, as the descendants of Isaac by Jacob, who was later known as Israel, the Israelites.[5] There is a Quranic term, *millat Ibrahim*, meaning 'religion of Ibrahim'[6] indicating that the Islamic religion sees itself as standing in a tradition of religious practice from Abraham.[7] The three monotheists religious traditions, Judaism, Christianity and Islam, have more in common than in contention. All three believe God is one, unique and concerned with humanity's condition. Each takes up the narrative of the others' Christianity and Islam carrying forward the story begun in the Hebrew scriptures of ancient Israel that defines Judaism.

Judaism in Relation to Christianity and Islam

Judaism has received many contradictory foundational dates by scholars. Some informed scholars have concluded that it is not a religion that can precisely be given an accurate date of foundation. Some attribute its origin to words of God that: "If you will be my people, I will be your God" (Exodus 6:7). But historical notices have shown that even before this request, there were some other intimate conversations between God and the Israelites. It is, however, strongly noted that the origins of Judaism lie in the Bronze Age polytheistic ancient Semitic religions, specifically Canaanite religions with elements of Babylonian religions and of the worship of Yahweh reflected in the early prophetic books of the Hebrew Bible. During the 1st (first) Iron Age, the Israelite religion became distinct from other Canaanite religions due to the unique monolatristic (proto-monotheistic) worship of Yahweh.[8] This means there were other religions in Canaan before the Israelites came to the land.

---

[5]Saheeh al-Bukharee, Book 55, hadith no. 584; Book 56, hadith no. 710.

[6]Derrida 2002, p. 3.

[7]The Quran, albaqarah; v. 135.

[8]Origins of Judaism. In Wikipedia Retrieved 31 July, 2018

The archetypal form of Judaism that existed since the 6th Century BC was Rabbinic Judaism after the codification of the Talmud. Rabbinic Judaism attained predominance with the Jews in Diaspora between the 2nd and the 6th Centuries with the development of the oral law and the Talmud in order to mitigate the interpretation of the Jewish scripture especially the Masoretic[9] and to encourage the practice of Judaism in the absence of Temple sacrifice and other practices no longer possible, while waiting for the Third Temple.[10]

According to Cohen (1999), Judaism is an ancient religion that started with the Jews. It is a monotheistic, Abrahamic religion with the Torah as its foundational text.[11] It encompasses the religion, philosophy and the cultural activities of the Jewish people.[12] Judaism is considered by religious Jews to be the expression of the covenant that God established with the Children of Israel. It incorporates a wide quantity of texts, practices, theological teachings, positions, and strong forms of organisation. The Torah is part of the larger text known as the *Tanakh* or the Hebrew Bible, and supplemental oral tradition represented by later texts such as the *Midrah*[13] and the Talmud.[14] The Torah is regarded as the five Books of Moses which are given ultimate respect by the Jews because they take instructions from the Torah.

---

[9]The authoritative Hebrew and Aramaic text of the Tanakh for Rabbinic Judaism. It was primarily copied, edited and distributed by a group of Jews known as the Masoretes between the 7th and 10th centuries CE.

[10] Origins of Judaism in Wikipedia Retrieved 31 July, 2018

[11]Shaye J.D. Cohen (1999). The Beginnings of Jewishness: Boundaries, Varieties, Uncertainties, Berkeley: University of California Press; p. 7

[12]Jacobs, Louis *(2007). "Judaism".In Fred Skolnik.*Encyclopaedia Judaica. *11 (2d ed.). Farmington Hills, Mich.: Thomson Gale. p. 511*

[13]The genre of rabbinic literature which contains early interpretations and commentaries on the Written Torah and Oral Torah (spoken law and sermons), as well as non-legalistic rabbinic literature (aggadah) and occasionally the Jewish religious laws (halakha), which usually form a running commentary on specific passages in the Hebrew Scripture

[14] The central text of Rabbinic Judaism and the primary source of Jewish religious law and theology

As a religion that started with the people of Israel, Judaism has its origins in the Kingdom of Judah and in Second Temple Judaism.[15] It has three essential and related elements namely: study of the written Torah (the books of Genesis, Exodus, Leviticus, Numbers, and Deuteronomy); the recognition of Israel (defined as the descendants of Abraham through his grandson Jacob) as a people elected by God as recipients of the law at Mount Sinai, his chosen people; and the requirement that Israel live in accordance with God's laws as given in the Torah.[16] The Israelites accepted God to be their Father and them His sons.

With this Father Son relationship, the Israelites developed a pattern of worship. There are a variety of movements in Judaism, most of which emerged from Rabbinic Judaism and maintain that God revealed his laws and commandments to Moses on Mount Sinai in the form of both the Written and Oral Torah.[17] Historically, this assertion was challenged by various groups or sects such as the Sadducees and Hellenistic Judaism during the Second Temple period; the Karaites and Sabbateans during the early and later medieval period.[18]

However, these challenges by Jewish sects did not stop the development of the Judaism. Today, the largest Jewish religious movements are Orthodox Judaism (Haredi Judaism and Modern Orthodox Judaism), Conservative Judaism, and Reform Judaism. The most important differences between these groups are their methodologies and styles to Jewish law, the authority of the rabbinic tradition, and the significance of the State of Israel.[19] Orthodox Judaism maintains and propagate that the Torah and Jewish law are divine in origin,

---

[15]Neusner 1992, p. 3.

[16]Ibid

[17]*"What is the oral Torah?"in Torah.org*. Retrieved 22 August 2010.

[18]*"Karaite Jewish University" in Kjuonline.com.Archived from the original on 25 August 2010.Retrieved* 22 August *2018.*

[19]*"Jewish Denominations".Religion Facts*.Retrieved 22 August 2018.

eternal and unchangeable; and that they should be strictly followed. Conservative and Reform Judaism are more liberal, with Conservative Judaism generally promoting a more traditionalist interpretation of Judaism's requirements than Reform Judaism.

A typical Reform position is that Jewish laws should be viewed as a set of general guidelines rather than restrictions and obligations whose observance is required of all Jews.[20] The laws were meant to direct and guide the Jews in everything they did. Historically, special courts enforced Jewish laws. To this day, these courts still exist, while the practice of Judaism, like any other religion is mostly voluntary as not every Jew practices the religion. Authority on theological and legal matters is not vested in any person or organization, but in the sacred texts and the rabbis and scholars who interpret them.[21] The interpretations may be new due to advancement in societal discoveries, but the original dictates of the law still in some way hold sway.

The acceptability of the interpretation of the sacred texts by the rabbis is universal among the Hebrews. Judaism is, therefore, considered the oldest monotheistic religions by many scholars. The Hebrews and Israelites were already referred to as "Jews" in later books of the *Tanakh* such as the Book of Esther with the term 'Jews' replacing the title "Children of Israel."[22] Judaism's texts, traditions and values greatly influenced the Abrahamic religions, including Christianity, Islam and the Baha'i Faith.[23] Many facets of Judaism have also directly or indirectly influenced secular Western ethics, civil laws and society. Hebraism was just as important a factor in the ancient development of Western civilisation as Hellenism and

---

[20] *"What is Reform Judaism?"in Reformjudaism.org*. Retrieved 22 August 2018.

[21] *"Judaism 101: Rabbis, Priests and Other Religious Functionaries" in Jewfaq.org*.Retrieved 22 August 2018.

[22] Wylen, S. M. (2000). Settings of silver: an introduction to Judaism.Paulist Press.

[23] *HeribertBusse (1998). Islam, Judaism, and Christianity: Theological and HistoricalAffiliations. Markus Wiener Publishers. pp. 63–112.*

Judaism; just as the background of Christianity and other subsequent religions, has considerably shaped Western ideals and morality since Early Christianity.[24] Some of the beliefs and practices of Judaism have been inadvertently inculcated into secular society, their traditional forms of celebrating some feasts being absorbed and modernised.

Judaism and Christianity

Judaism is generally regarded as an offshoot of Christianity, and there are many obvious reasons to claim so. It was originally a sect of Second Temple Judaism,[25] but the two religions diverged in the first century. The historical annals show that the differences between Christianity and Judaism originally centred on whether or not Jesus was the Jewish Messiah but it eventually became irreconcilable. Major noticeable differences between the two faiths include the nature of the Messiah, of atonement and sin, the status of God's commandments to the people of Israel, and perhaps most significantly of the nature of God himself. As a result of these differences Judaism traditionally regards Christianity as *Shituf* or worship of the God of Israel in a much different way that is not monotheistic. Christianity has traditionally regarded Judaism as obsolete with the invention of Christianity and Jews as a people replaced by the Church, though a Christian belief in dual-covenant theology[26] emerged as a phenomenon following Christian reflection on how their theology influenced the Nazi Holocaust.[27] This understanding poses numerous traditional and theological arguments between the two Abrahamic religions.

---

[24] Cambridge University Historical Series, An Essay on Western Civilization in Its Economic Aspects, p.40:

[25] Judaism between the construction of the Second Temple in Jerusalem, c. 515 BCE, and its destruction by the Romans in 70 CE

[26] A school of thought in Christianity regarding the relevance of the Hebrew Bible, which Christians call the Old Testament.

[27] Kendall S. R. (1996). The God of Israel and Christian Theology, Minneapolis: Fortress.

Since the Middle Ages, the Catholic Church upheld the *Constitution pro Judaeis* (Formal Statement on the Jews), which stated thusly: We decree that no Christian shall use violence to force them to be baptised, so long as they are unwilling and refuse. ... Without the judgment of the political authority of the land, no Christian shall presume to wound them or kill them or rob them of their money or change the good customs that they have thus far enjoyed in the place where they live.[28] This constitution was meant to make Christianity a free religion; a religion without coercion. Any Jew who wanted to be a Christian was to decide by himself without any external force from the Christian community.

The modern attitude of Christians toward the Jewish people and Judaism has positively changed since World War II. Pope John Paul II and the Catholic Church have "upheld the Church's acceptance of the continuing and permanent election of the Jewish people" as well as a reaffirmation of the covenant between God and the Jews.[29] The closeness between the two monotheistic religions has become palpable that some references, especially biblical interpretations of some passages, from both the Old and New Testaments are drawn in order to ascertain their supposed divine link.

The Link between Judaism and Christianity

Isaiah 51:1, 2 "Listen to me, you who follow after righteousness, you who seek the Lord: Look to the rock from which you were hewn, And to the hole of the pit from which you were dug. Look to Abraham your father, And to Sarah who bore you; for I called him alone, and blessed him and increased him."

"Jesus was a Jew. His teachings, like those of his followers, reflect a distinct ethnicity and culture. The evidence found in

---

[28] *Baskin, J.R.; Seeskin, K. (2010).The Cambridge Guide to Jewish History, Religion, and Culture.Cambridge University Press. p. 120*

[29] ^*Wigoder, G. (1988). Jewish-Christian Relations Since the Second World War. Manchester University Press. p. 87*

the New Testament is abundantly clear: as a mother gives birth and nourishes a child, so Hebrew culture and language gave birth to and nourishes Christianity."[30] These relations still abound and the two religions seem to have more that unites than divides them.

Abraham is known to be the first Jew or Hebrew. Jews and the sect (Christianity) led by the son of Joseph the Carpenter, Jesus, are from the seed of Abraham. "Also, if you belong to the Messiah, you are seed of Abraham and heirs according to the promise." Gal. 3:29. Gal 3:8 says he was the first Christian (believer of the same gospel), being preached to by God Himself.

The Old Testament is a Holy Book used by both adherents of Judaism and Christianity. It was penned down by Jews who received revelation from God through the power and inspiration of the Holy Spirit. The New Testament was also written by Jews with the exception of the Gospel of Luke. Judaism does not need Christianity to explain its existence, but Christianity needs the former in order to explicate its existence. Christianity, therefore, definitely needs Judaism to expound its survival history and what it believes in. In history, Christianity is known or has been dubbed as the 'Judeo-Christian faith'.

There were numerous sects among the Jewish society, including the Zealots, Hassideans, the Pharisees, the Sadducees and many others before the advent of Christianity. The followers of the son of Joseph the Carpenter known as 'Jesus' only came to be known as Christians in Antioch in AD 42, (Acts 21:17-26). Prior to this time, they were known as 'the sect of the Nazarenes'. The selected Apostles were all Jews. Paul was a Torah-observant Jew (Acts 21:17-26).

Jesus says in John 4:22: "You people don't know what you are worshipping; we worship what we do know, because salvation comes from the Jews." The salvation history started with the Patriarch Abraham. God made promises to Abraham, and the promises of the Abrahamic Covenant have been entrusted to his descendants, the Jews. From the Jews we have the patriarchs, the prophets, the apostles, the Bible and the Saviour! In you (Abraham) shall all families of the earth be blessed." (Gen. 12:3). "... in you and in your seed shall all the families of the earth be blessed." (Gen 28:14).

In Eph. 2:12-13 it is stated: "At that time you had no Messiah. You were estranged from the national life of Israel. You were foreigners to the covenants embodying God's promise. You were in this world without hope and without God. But now, you who were once far off have been brought near through the shedding of the Messiah's blood." Also in Eph. 3:6 it is written, "that in union with the Messiah and through the Good News the Gentiles were to be joint heirs, a joint body and joint sharers with the Jews in what God has promised."

St. Paul was a Jew who did not deny his Jewishness. "In that case, I say, isn't it that they have stumbled with the result that they have permanently fallen away? Heaven forbid! Quite the contrary, it is by means of their stumbling that the deliverance has come to the Gentiles, in order to provoke them to jealousy...For if their casting aside Jesus means reconciliation for the world, what will their accepting him mean? It will be life from the dead! And you - a wild olive - were grafted in among them and have become equal sharers in the rich root of the olive tree, then don't boast..."(Romans 11:16-24).

Jesus respected the Law as a Jew and encouraged his followers to do the same. It is clear from the Gospels that Jesus had a reputation as a Jewish rabbi (Mark 14:45; John 1:38). Peter (Mark 9:5) and Mary Magdalene (John 20:16) both referred to Jesus as "Rabbi." Moreover, the Jewish ruler, Nicodemus thought that this title was appropriate for Jesus: "Rabbi, we know that you are a teacher who has come from God. For no one could perform the signs you are doing if God were not with him" (John 3:2). Jesus clearly affirmed the Torah when He said: "Do not think that I have come to abolish the Law or the Prophets; I have not come to abolish them but to fulfill them. For truly I tell you, until heaven and earth disappear, not the smallest letter, not the least stroke of a pen, will by any means disappear from the Law until everything is accomplished. Jesus did not abolish Judaism but He reformed Judaism (Heb 9:10). Many Jews could not accept this form of reform by Jesus, thus opening the way for his Gospel to be preached to the Gentiles who gladly received it.

Judaism and Islam

Both Judaism and Islam have their roots from the patriarch Abraham, and they are, therefore, considered Abrahamic religions. In both Jewish and Muslim traditions, the Jews and Arabs are descendants of the two sons of Abraham, Isaac and Ishmael, respectively. The firstborn son of Abraham is Ishmael, and he is considered by Muslims as the *Father of the Arabs*. Abraham's second son Isaac is known to be the *Father of the Hebrews*.

While both religions are monotheistic and share many commonalities, they differ based on the fact that Jews do not consider Jesus or Mohammad to be prophets. The adherents of these religions have interacted since the 7th century when Islam originated and spread in the Arabian Peninsula. Indeed, the years from 712 to 1066 CE were considered the Golden Age of Jewish culture in Spain under the Ummayad and the Abbasid rulers. Non-Muslim monotheists living in these countries, including Jews, were known as *dhimmis*. Dhimmis were allowed to practice their own religions and administer their own internal affairs, but they were subject to certain restrictions that were not imposed on Muslims.[31] For example, they had to pay the *jizya*, a per capita tax imposed on free adult non-Muslim males,[32] and they were also forbidden to bear arms or testify in court cases involving Muslims.[33]

---

[31] Lewis (1984), pp. 10,

[32] Ibid

[33] Lewis (1984), pp. 9.

Moses is mentioned in the Quran more than any other individual, and his life is narrated and recounted more than that of any other prophet.[34] In the Islamic Holy Book, there are about 43 references to the Jews (excluding individual prophets)[35] and many are also found in the Hadith.

Islam was substantially influenced by Judaism in its fundamental religious outlook, structure, jurisprudence and practice.[36] Because of this similarity, as well as the influence of Muslim culture and philosophy on the Jewish community within the Islamic world, there has been considerable and continued physical, theological, and political overlap between the two religions. For instance the first Islamic Wagf[37] was donated by a Jew, Rabbi Mukhayriq.[38]

The Prophet Muhammad while proselytising in Mecca, initially considered Christians and Jews (both of whom he referred to as " People of the Book") as natural allies, sharing the core principles of his teachings, and anticipated their acceptance and support.[39] Muhammad, since Judaism was already in practice, adopted some features of the Jewish worship and customs such as fasting on the Yom Kippur day. According to Alford Welch, (Professor of Arabic and Islamic Studies), the Jewish practice of having three daily prayer rituals appears to have been a factor in the introduction of the Islamic midday prayer. Muhammad's adoption of the practice of facing north towards Jerusalem which is Islam's first

---

[34] Annabel Keeler, "Moses from a Muslim Perspective", in: Solomon, Norman; Harries, Richard; Winter, Tim (eds.), Abraham's children: Jews, Christians, and Muslims in conversation, by. T&T Clark Publ. (2005), pp. 55–66.

[35] Yahud, Encyclopedia of Islam

[36] Prager, D; Telushkin, J. Why the Jews?: The Reason for Antisemitism. New York: Simon & Schuster, 1983. pp. 110–26.

[37] An inalienable charitable endowment under Islamic law. It typically means donating a building, plot of land or other assets for Muslim religious or charitable purposes with no intention of reclaiming the assets.

[38] Muqtedar Khan (4 December 2009). "Mukhayriq 'the best of the Jews'"

[39] https://en.wikipedia.org/wiki/Islam

Qiblah or direction of prayer and later changed to facing the Kabah in Mecca was also practiced among other groups in Arabia.[40]

The Prophet's departure from earlier religions such as Judaism and Christianity rather emphasised it close roots to Judaism. Islam, according to some Muslims, is merely the latest expression of the Abrahamic tradition which is rooted in Judaism. The language and ethos of Islam is similar to aspects of ancient Judaism. Mohammad is a prophet who stans in the direct line of prophets stretching from Abraham and Moses through the ancient Hebrew Prophets Isaiah and Jeremiah.[41]

Islam also retains the universalistic message of Judaism and Christianity while tightening the social boundaries of its faith community. There is, however, a slight shift because Islam's tribe is not one of biological inheritance like Judaism but a spiritual family, the Ummah.[42]

Christianity and Islam

The influence of Christianity on Islam is as old as Islam itself. This could be traced back to Eastern Christianity which involves Christian traditions and Church families that originally developed during the classical and late antiquity in the Middle East, Egypt, Northeast Africa, Eastern Europe, Asia Minor, the Malabar Coast of Southern India, and parts of the Far East that surrounded the origins of Islam.[43] Through the relationship that existed between Christians and the Arabs before the formation of Islam, the former introduced the Arab Muslims to Greek learning. Eastern Christians (particularly the Nestorian Christians) contributed to the Arab Islamic civilisation during the Ummayad and the Abbasid periods by

---

[40] https://en.wikipedia.org/wiki/Islamic%E2%80%93Jewish_relations

[41] www.us.sagepub.com

[42] www.us.sagepub.com

[43] Michael Nazir-Ali. Islam, a Christian perspective, Westminster John Knox Press, 1983, p. 66

translating works of Greek philosophers to Syriac and afterwards to Arabic.[44] They also influenced Islam in the area of arts, culture, science and medicine.[45]

Judeo-Christian perspective holds the view that Islam originated with Muhammad who borrowed heavily from both rabbinical Judaism and Christianity. Concerning the alleged borrowing from Christianity, it is traditionally held that Muhammad most frequently took from the teachings of the Eastern churches and from a variety of apocryphal Christian writings. Thus, from the Judeo-Christian perspective, Islam originated in the Seventh Century CE as an amalgamation of Judaism and Christianity.

On the aspect of prayer, academics state that Islam was substantially influenced by Christianity and Judaism the religions that were common in the Middle East during the time of Muhammad.[46] Muslim pray five times a day, a practice that has its origins in the canonical hours of Christians, especially those used in the 4th Century by believers of the Oriental Orthodox Churches (that were widely regarded as Monophysite) who prayed seven times a day. The extensive contact that Muhammad and his companions had with Syrian Christian Monks influenced this practice.[47] History records that Abubakar and other early contemporaries of Muhammad were exposed to these fixed times of prayer of the Christians in Syria and it is not unlikely that they relayed their observations to Muhammad, "placing the potential for Christian influence directly within the Prophet's circle of followers and leaders."[48] It is not doubtful that Muhammad who had direct contact with

---

[44] Hill, Donald. Islamic Science and Engineering.1993. Edinburgh Univ. Press.ISBN 0-7486-0455-3, p.4

[45] https://en.wikipedia.org/wiki/Christian_influences_in_Islam

[46] Heinz, Justin Paul (2008). The Origins of Muslim Prayer: Sixth and Seventh Century Religious Influences on the Salat Ritual. University of Missouri-Columbia. p. 115, 123, 125, 133, 141-142.

[47] Ibid

[48] Ibid

the Christians of Najrān in Yemen, would have been influenced by the Christian practice of facing the east while praying, which was ubiquitous in Christendom at the time.[49] Also, the position of prostration used by the Desert Fathers, Coptic Christian Monks of Egypt, may have influenced the position of Sujjud, marked by the Quranic symbol.[50] The Quran assumes familiarity with major narratives which widely recounted in the Jewish and Christian scriptures by summarising some, dwelling at length on others and differing in others.[51]

[49] Ibid

[50] Ibid

[51] Wheeler, Brannon M. (2002). Prophets in the Quran: an introduction to the Quran and Muslim exegesis. Continuum.p. 15.

CHAPTER TWO

MONOTHEISM

"

Monotheism, belief in the existence of one god, or in the oneness of God. As such, it is distinguished from polytheism, the belief in the existence of many gods, from atheism, the belief that there is no god, and from agnosticism, the belief that the existence or nonexistence of a god or of gods is unknown or unknowable. Monotheism characterizes the traditions of Judaism, Christianity, and Islam, and elements of the belief are discernible in numerous other religions
- Encyclopedia Britannica

Abrahamic religions are acclaimed monotheistic. They believe in the existence of One God. History has shown that there was a departure from Polytheism to Monotheism, Polytheism was exalted before monotheism. Judaism that is popularly considered the first monotheistic religion is an offshoot of Polytheism. The history of how monotheism became pervasive and expanded beyond Judaism is complex because it has both historical and archaeological information. The rise of monotheism has been influenced by societal experiences. The diverse ancient gods proved inconsequential to the needs and demands of the Jewish people until a certain unseen god intervened in their lives and proved to be accessible especially at their time of need. This was after the period of the exile in Babylon.

In light of the foregoing, this chapter discusses the transition from Polytheism to Monotheism and will attempt to show how these monotheistic religions have fared. There are among them similarities in forms of worship, attributes to God and the acknowledgement of the supremacy of God. We shall also see some differences in their methods of approach to God and how their relationship with God should be channeled.

Polytheism to Monotheism

Judaism is traditionally considered the oldest monotheistic religions in the world. It is understood by scholars that there existed among the earlier Israelites the worship of many gods before they finally came to acknowledge one God and denied the existence of others. God in later Judaism was strictly monotheistic, an absolute one, indivisible, and incomparable being, who is the ultimate cause of all existence. The Babylonian Talmud references other "foreign gods" as non-existent entities to whom humans mistakenly ascribe reality and power.[52] One of the best-known statements of Rabbinical Judaism on monotheism is the Second of Maimonides' 13 Principles of faith namely: "I believe by complete faith that the Creator, blessed be His name, is a Unity, and there is no union in any way like Him. He alone is our God, who was, who is, and who is to be." Given that Judaism is seen as the leading religion among the Abrahamic religions, it is only appropriate to see how they concept of a monotheistic God was developed.

During the 8th Century BCE, the worship of Yahweh in Israel was in competition with many other cults, described by the Yahwist faction collectively as Baals. The oldest books of the Hebrew Bible reflect this competition, as in the books of Hosea and Nahum, whose authors lament the "apostasy" of the people of Israel, threatening them with the wrath of God if they do not give up their polytheistic cults.[53]

Ancient Israelite religion was originally polytheistic.[54] The Israelites worshipped many deities, including El, Baal, Asherah, and Astarte. Yahweh was originally the national god of the kingdom of Israel and the kingdom of Judah. As time

[52]Babylonian Talmud, Megilla 7b-17a.

[53]Othmar, K.; Uehlinger, C. (1998). Gods, Goddesses, and Images of God in Ancient Israel, Fortress Press and 1 Kings 18, Jeremiah 2

[54]*Albertz, Rainer (1994).* A History of Israelite Religion, Volume I: From the Beginnings to the End of the Monarchy. *Westminster John Knox.p. 61.*

progressed, the henotheistic[55] cult of Yahweh grew increasingly militant in its opposition to the worship of other gods.[56] Later, the reforms of King Josiah imposed a form of strict Israeli monolatrism. After the fall of Judah and the beginning of the Babylonian captivity, a small circle of priests and scribes gathered around the exiled royal court, where they first developed the concept of Yahweh as the sole God of the world.[57] And from there continued the idea of a monotheistic god or God which later spread among the people.

Some scholars like Albright maintain that monotheistic concept of God started with Moses, from his encounter with Yahweh at Mount Sinai. This kind of monotheism is generally referred to as 'Mosaic monotheism'.[58] The first and second of the commandments that Moses received from Yahweh, prohibited the veneration of any other divinity apart from Yahweh (Exod 20:1-4).

Given the recognition that started to be ascribed to the monotheistic God, Judaism began getting a firm footing. And this gave rise to the general believed that monotheism could have originated with the Mosaic age, making Moses the first monotheist. Langdon (1976), who was known to be a supporter of an early monotheism in Israel, while admitting that subsequent Israelite religion was no longer monotheistic but rather syncretistic or polytheistic, argues that Israelite religion was monotheistic from Israel's earliest existence in the ancient Near Eastern world. He believes that the history of religion was a decline from monotheism to extreme polytheism. He cites the Sumerian religion dating back to 3000 BCE, and argues that the Sumerians back then had a total of 750 gods but that they ended up having about 5000 gods a millennium later. This incident, according to him, is confirmation that Israelite

---

[55]Henotheism is the worship of a single god while not denying the existence or possible existence of other deities.

[56]Ibid

[57]*Gnuse, Robert Karl (1 May 1997).* No Other Gods: Emergent Monotheism in Israel. *Sheffield Academic Press.p. 225.*

[58]Albright, *Stone Age to Christianity*, 257-72.

religion has been declining from its early monotheism to polytheism. To be assertive in his position, Langdon writes:

> I may fail to carry conviction in concluding that both in Sumerian and Semitic religions, monotheism preceded polytheism... The evidence and reasons for this conclusion, so contrary to accepted and current views, have been set down with care and with the perception of adverse criticism.[59]

Some other advocates of the early monotheistic view maintain that monotheism started during the monarchical era. This includes scholars like Smith, Lang and McCarter.[60] Some of the monotheistic expressions in the monarchical era occurred during the time of the reforms of Kings Hezekiah (715-687 BCE) and Josiah (640-609 BCE) who advocated for an exclusive worship of Yahweh. It was also during the monarchical period that the "Yahweh-Alone" movement which advocated for an exclusive worship of Yahweh[61] emerged. The Yahweh-Alone movement, apart from other practices, also condemned the use of images in Israelite religion.[62]

After the emphasis on the exclusive worship of Yahweh, the exilic period was also seen by some of the advocates of monotheism as the "formative" stage of what would later become pure monotheism.[63] On his part, Smith (2004) opines that the exilic era was the time during which "Israel explicitly denied the power of all other deities.[64]" Baly (1970), another scholar holds that pure monotheism only became a reality

[59]Langdon, (1976), *Semitic Mythology*, xviii; cf. Arthur C. Custance, *Evolution OR Creation* (Grand Rapids, MI: Zondervan Publishing House, 113-14.

[60]Morton S. (1987), Palestinian Parties and Politics that Shaped the Old Testament. London: SCM Press, 23

[61]See Mark S. Smith (2004). The Memoirs of God: History, Memory, and the Experience of the Divine in Ancient Israel. Minneapolis: Fortress Press, 60-61.

[62]Dirk J. H. (1999). Aspects of Monotheism: A Continued Debate," OTE 12.3 498-500.

[63]Baruch H. (2009). From Gods to God: The Dynamic of Iron Age Cosmologies (ed. M.J. Adams, FAT, 63; Tubigen: Mohr Siebeck, 13-56; W. Eichrodt, Theology of the Old Testament (vol. 1, trans. J.A. Bakker, OTL; London: SCM, 1961), 220-27, 363-64; and Smith, Early History, 3.

[64]Smith, Early History, 3.

under Deutero- Isaiah in the exilic period. He however, believes that monotheism started out of a steady process which began at Sinai where Israel formed a covenant with Yahweh.

Succeeding Prophets including Elijah and Amos continued to build on the Sinaitic foundation which was eventually embraced by Deutero- Isaiah in the exile.[65] Although with quality differences in monumental details, most of the proponents of late monotheism side with Baly that exclusive monotheism was finally achieved after series of events.

In a related development, Morton (1952) argues that monotheism was preceded by several reforms aimed at the exclusivity of Yahweh in pre exilic Israel. Some of these reforms included those promulgated by prophets and the Deuteronomists, the Yahweh-Alone movement, as well as the reforms of Hezekiah and Josiah. Morton further argues, however, that pure monotheism only came during the exilic and post-exilic periods following the initial influence of Deutero-Isaiah.[66]

Smith (2004) traces the origin of monotheism through the processes of convergence and differentiation.[67] Under the model of convergence, we almost cannot discuss any aspect of Israelite religion in isolation from Israel's Canaanite background. Israelite religion in its early stages included some Canaanite features incorporating the veneration of El, Baal, and Asherah; as well as other cultic practices at the high places, and devotion to the dead.

Subsequently, through the ancient practice in which divinities were raised to state or national status in most cultures, Israelite

---

[65]Baly, D. (1970). "The Geography of Monotheism," in Translating and Understanding the Old Testament: Essays in Honor of Herbert Gordon May (eds. H.T. Frank and W. Reed; Nashville: Abingdon Press, 253-78

[66]Morton S. (1952). The Common Theology of the Ancient Near East," JBL 71 135-47; idem, "Religious Parties Among the Exiles Before 587," in Palestinian Parties and Politics that Shaped the Old Testament (New York: Columbia University Press, 1971), 15-56.

[67]Smith, *Early History*, 195-99.

religion skewed towards monolatry.[68] Through the model of differentiation, Israelite religion went through a transformation and had to be separated from its Canaanite past. Differentiation operated through what Petersen characterised as "evolution" and "revolution."[69] Israel had to throw out some Canaanite practices as her religion gradually grew towards monolatry and ultimately monotheism. It was Israel's insistence on a single deity that eventually distinguished her from all the surrounding traditions. Describing the development of monolatry and monotheism, and how they were achieved through the processes of evolution and revolution, Smith (2004) summarises as follows:

> It was an "evolution" in two respects. Monolatry grew out of an early, limited Israelite polytheism that was not strictly discontinuous with that of its Iron Age neighbours. Furthermore, adherence to one deity was a changing reality within the period of the Judges and the Monarchy in Israel. While evolutionary in character, Israelite monolatry was also "revolutionary" in a number of respects. The process of differentiation and the eventual displacement of Baal from Israel's national cult distinguished Israel's religion from the religions of its neighbours.[70]

What, therefore, we may consider as pure monotheism, according to Smith, only came to be known around the sixth and fifth centuries. It is evident that monotheism, which is the belief in one God while denying the existence of all other gods, has been the subject of a long standing debate, and we might add that it continues to be a contentious issue.

Monotheism in Judaism

In Judaism, God, the Cause of all in the universe, is one. This does not mean one as in one of a pair, nor one like a species

---

[68]Monolatry is belief in the existence of many gods but with the consistent worship of only one deity.

[69]Petersen, "Israel and Monotheism," 92-107.

[70]Smith, *Early History*, 198

(which encompasses many individuals), nor one as in an object that is made up of many elements, nor as a single simple object that is infinitely divisible. Rather, God is a unity unlike any other possible unity.[71] The idea of God as a duality or trinity is heretical in Judaism because it is considered akin to polytheism. Judaism maintains that any teaching that portrays the existence of an intermediary between humanity and God is traditionally considered heretical. Maimonides writes that:

> God is the only one we may serve and praise....We may not act in this way toward anything beneath God, whether it be an angel, a star, or one of the elements... There are no intermediaries between us and God. All our prayers should be directed towards God; nothing else should even be considered.[72]

In reference to this, some rabbinic scholars objected the stand of Maimonides. Nachmanides[73] maintains that it is acceptable to seek the mediation of the angels to beseech God on our behalf. This argument manifests notably in the Selichot prayer called "Machnisay Rachamim", a request to the angels to intercede with God.[74]

Hence, monotheism in Judaism is more than the belief in one God, but a unique way of viewing and understanding the world as the 'art work' of God. Since there is no intermediary between God and man, it, therefore, means that whatever happens in the world demonstrates that God is ever-present in people's lives. Every sight they see, sound they hear and experience is meeting with God through other means. Thus, Judaism uses the term *shituf* to refer to the worship of God in a manner which it deems to be neither purely monotheistic (though still permissible for

---

[71]Yesode Ha-Torah 1:7

[72]Maimonides, 13 principles of faith, Fifth Principle

[73]Moses ben Nahman, commonly known as Nachmanides, and also referred to by the acronym Ramban and by the contemporary nickname Bonastruc ça Porta, was a leading medieval Jewish scholar, Sephardic rabbi, philosopher, physician, kabbalist, and biblical commentator.

[74]God in Judaism in https://en.wikipedia.org/wiki/Retrieved 22.06.2020

non-Jews) nor polytheistic (which would be prohibited).[75] What is this total belief in One God? The Shema explains.

The Shema

Shema Yisrael ("Hear, O Israel") is a Jewish prayer, and it is the first two words of a section of the Torah. It is the title of a prayer that serves as a centre-piece of the morning and evening Jewish prayer services. The first verse encapsulates the monotheistic essence of Judaism: "Hear, O Israel: the LORD our God, the LORD is one" as found in Deuteronomy 6:4. In Judaism, the Shema is considered to be the most important part of their prayer service and its twice-daily recitation as a *mitza* (religious commandment). Also, it is traditional for Jews to say the Shema as their last words, and for parents to teach their children to say it before they go to sleep at night.

The Shema includes and emphasises several different ideas such as:

> There is only ONE God. These words give expression to Israel's deep conviction of the existence of one indivisible God through whose will the universe and all contained in it was created.

God is a UNITY. He is a single, whole, complete indivisible entity. He cannot be divided into parts or described by attributes. Any attempt to ascribe attributes to God is merely man's imperfect attempt to understand the infinite. Also, God is the only being to whom we should offer praise.

God in Judaism is known to be the sole CREATOR of the universe; speculated to be Omnipotent, Omniscient and omnipresent. Maimonides among other rabbinical authorities describes God thusly: "The foundation of all foundations and the pillar of wisdom is to know that there is a Primary Being who brought into being all existence. All the beings of the

---

[75] *Jacobs, Louis, ed. (1995).* The Jewish Religion: A Companion 1st Edition. *Oxford University Press. pp. 79–80*

heavens, the earth, and what is between them came into existence only from the truth of His being."[76] We shall now see a few of the human attributes of God.

God as Creator

In Genesis 1:1 it is stated that "in the beginning God created the heaven and the earth." Everything in the universe is believed to have been created by God. Judaism completely rejects the dualistic notion that evil was created by Satan or some other deity. All comes from God. As Isaiah said, "I am the LORD, and there is none else. I form the light and create darkness, I make peace and create evil. I am the LORD that does all these things" (Isaiah 45:6-7).

God is Omnipotent

God in Judaism is believed to possess the capacity to do anything. It is said that the only thing that is beyond His control is the fear of Him, that is, He has given us free will, and He does not compel us to do His will. This belief in God's omnipotence has been sorely tested during the many persecutions of the Jews. Some Jews explain and maintain that God has a reason for allowing things to happen, even if we in our limited perception and understanding cannot see the reason.

Jews often describe God as omnipotent. Some modern Jewish theologians, for example, Claussen (2010) has argued that God is not omnipotent and have found many biblical and classical sources to support this view.[77]

God is Omniscience

The omniscience of God is expressed by two names of God found in the Hebrew Scriptures. The first is found in 1 Samuel 2:3: The Lord is a "God of Knowledge" (*El De'ot*). The Mighty One is all knowing and is the source of all knowledge. The

---

[76]Mishneh Torah, book HaMadda', section Yesodei ha-Torah, chapter 1:1

[77]Claussen G. (2010). "God and Suffering in Heschel's Torah Min Ha-Shamayim". Conservative Judaism 61, no. 4 p. 17

second name is found in Genesis 22:14. God is called "the Lord Who Sees" (*Adonai Yireh*). The Lord sees everything. He is absolutely aware of the needs of His people and will see to it that they are provided for. God's omniscience is taught throughout the Holy Scriptures. For instance, with Him is wisdom and might; to Him belong counsel and understanding (Job 12:13) Psalm 94:9 declares: He that made the ear, shall He not hear? He that formed the eye, shall He not see?

To say that God is omniscient is that He possesses perfect knowledge and therefore has no need to learn anything. It means that God has never learned anything, and cannot learn. Cf. Isaiah 40:13-*14* and Romans 11:34.

There has been some high level of disagreement on the 'omniscientship' of God by some prominent medieval Jewish philosophers. For instance, Gersonides argues that God knows the choices open to each individual, but does not know the choices that an individual will make.[78] Abraham ibn Daud believes that God was not omniscient or omnipotent with respect to human action.[79] This boils down to the problem of evil in the world. If God knows all, why is there evil?

God is Omnipresent

God as the creator of everything, that is, He is believed to be everywhere. He is close to everything. He is next to everyone. He is bigger than the universe, and beyond it, and, yet, He is with each one.

All other created beings, including angels, are restricted to a given place at a given time. When they are here, they are not there. But God cannot be limited by space or time that He himself created. There can be no limits to His presence. There is no place beyond Him. He surrounds the finite creation and

---

[78]Jacobs, Louis *(1990). God, Torah, Israel: traditionalism without fundamentalism*. Cincinnati*: Hebrew Union College Press.*

[79]Guttmann, Julius *(1964). Philosophies of Judaism: The History of Jewish Philosophy from Biblical Times to Franz Rosenzweig*. New York City: Holt, Rinehart and Winston. *pp. 150–151.*

contains it. Rabbi Paul declares to the philosophers at Athens: In Him we live and move and have our being (Acts 17:28).

According to Hilde Bert[80]: "God is over all things under all things; outside all; within but not enclosed; without but not excluded; above but not raised up; below but not depressed; wholly above, presiding; wholly beneath, sustaining; wholly within, filling. As David said "Where can I go from Your Spirit? Or where can I flee from Your presence? If I ascend to heaven, You are there; if I make my bed in Sheol, behold, You are there. If I take the wings of the dawn, if I dwell in the remotest part of the sea, even there Your hand will lead me "(Psalm 139:7-10).

Monotheism in Christianity

God cannot be defined but be described because He is divine. Human attributes can only be employed in order to give a mental glimpse of him whom has not been seen. According to Christianity, God is the self-existent One, having no need of being created, since He has existed forever and is the cause of all things, including the dimension of space and time, to which He is not subject. Likewise, God is not subject to the physical creation, but is spiritual in nature, residing in the spiritual dimensions of heaven.[81]

God is the eternal being who created and preserves all things. Christians believe God to be both transcendent (wholly independent of, and removed from, the material universe) and immanent (involved in the world).[82] Christian teachings of the immanence and involvement of God and his love for humanity exclude the belief that God is of the same substance as the created universe[83] but accept that God's divine Nature was hypostatically united to human nature in the person of Jesus Christ, in an event known as the incarnation.

---

[80]A French ecclesiastic, hagiographer and theologian.

[81]Rich Deem. "Who is God" in.http://www.godandscience.org/doctrine.Retrieved 23/07/18

[82]Leith, J. H. (1992) Basic Christian Doctrine.

[83]Berkhof, L. (1963). Systematic Theology Banner of Truth publishers, p.61

Christians believe in one God and in the divinity of Jesus, as Paul says in 1 Corinthians 8:5-6: "For even if there are so-called gods, whether in heaven or on earth (as indeed there are many 'gods' and many 'lords'), yet for us there is but one God, the Father, from whom all things came and for whom we live; and there is but one Lord, Jesus Christ, through whom all things came and through whom we live."

In a similar vein, Irenaeus, writing in the 2nd Century postulates: "His greatness lacks nothing, but contains all things."[84]In the 8th century, John of Damascus listed eighteen attributes which remain widely accepted.[85]As time passed, theologians developed systematic lists of these attributes, some based on statements in the Bible (such as the Lord's Prayer, stating that the Father is in Heaven), others based on theological reasoning. The Kingdom of God is a prominent phrase in the Synoptic Gospels and while there is near unanimous agreement among scholars that it represents a key element of the teachings of Jesus, there is little scholarly agreement on its exact interpretation.[86]

God the Creator

The Christian Bible in Genesis (Torah) opens with the words "In the beginning God created the heavens and the earth" (Genesis 1:1). The Bible is clear on the foundational truth about God as the creator of all that is in the universe. The prophet Isaiah proclaims God as the Creator when he says, "Do you not know? Have you not heard? The Lord is the everlasting God, the Creator of the ends of the earth. He will not grow tired or weary, and his understanding no one can fathom." 40:28. All three Persons of the Trinity were involved in the creation of the universe (Genesis 1:2; Acts 17:24; Hebrews 1:2).

---

[84]Eric Francis Osborn. Irenaeus of Lyons

[85]William A. Dyrness, Veli-MattiKärkkäinen, Juan F. Martinez and Simon Chan. Global Dictionary of Theology

[86]France, R. T. (2003). ,Divine Government: God's Kingship in the Gospel of Mark.

A simple and conventional understanding of a creator is one who makes something new. A new thing is created or made out of an existing thing. God did not create out of an existing element, but through a word, and act of command: Let there be... People or co-creators can "create" things out of already existing things. Co-creators begin with preexisting materials and form it into new things. What is commonly called "creativity" is more akin to synthesis. God had no need for such raw assets to work with. He started with nothing (Colossians 1: 16).

Genesis 1:1 says that "in the beginning, God created the heavens and the earth." before creation therefore, there existed no heavens and no earth. God commanded them into being (Genesis 1:3, 6, 9). "In six days the Lord made the heavens and the earth, the sea, and all that is in them" (Exodus 20:11; cf. Revelation 10: 6). God the Creator is the absolute initiator and stylish of all things that are as the Psalmist puts it, "How many are your works, Lord! In wisdom you made them all" (Psalm 104:24).

Before God created man, He took some clay that He had already made and formed a man. Then He breathed His own life into that man, and "man became a living soul" (Genesis 2:7). When He created the first woman, Eve, He also used that which He had already made. He caused Adam to fall into a deep sleep and took a rib from his side and formed a woman (Genesis 2: 21). Man, therefore, was not created through a spoken word or a command. Man was created out of existing clay. Eve was also created out of an existing matter, man, because He cause Adam to fall into a deep sleep and took a rib from his side and formed woman.

The Creator is the Designer and Craftsman of all things in the universe. He created man and woman in his Image and likeness by breathing His own life into them, (Genesis 1:27). That means human beings are more like God than any other created thing. Humankind is specially made that it can reason, choose good or evil, and could love. Man has the capacity to express his emotions; he has intellect, and the power and desire to create things out of other existing things. God desires to have communion with humankind (Genesis 3:8-9; Jeremiah 29:12). He does not seek fellowship with other created things as he does with human beings, although He has absolute power and control over them.

It is important to note that the Creator was not created, God alone is the Creator. Man cannot truly create, (No need to go into the Big Bang saga here), because he must start with something that has already been created. Everything originated from God (Jeremiah 10:16; James 1:17; Revelation 10:6).

God is One

The Bible clearly says there is only one God. *"Hear, O Israel: The Lord our God, the Lord is one"* (Deuteronomy 6:4). At the same time, we encounter passages in the Bible that show the one God consisting of more persons. This may be hard to understand. It should, however, be realised that it is not because of a logical contradiction but because of human limitedness.

When the passages that talk about the plurality in God are understood in context, the clarity of three persons, God the Father, God the Son, and God the Holy Spirit becomes obtrusive and this is called the 'Trinity'. That the term 'Trinity' is not used in the Bible does not mean it is against the Bible or not found expressively in the Bible. The Trinitarian concept is obviously there in the Bible.

God Says "Let us make man in our image, according to our likeness; and let man have dominion over the fish of the sea, and over the birds of the air, and over the cattle, and over all the wild animals of the earth, and over every creeping thing that creeps upon the earth" (Genesis 1:26). The phrase "let us" gives the idea of plurality.

The phrase "let us" is again used elsewhere by God in Genesis. After Adam and Eve sinned the Bible records: Then the Lord

God said, "Behold, the man has become like one of US, knowing good and evil; and now, he might stretch out his hand, and take also from the tree of life, and eat, and live forever" (Genesis 3:22).

At the incident at the Tower of Babel, God says: Come, let US go down there and confuse their language, so that they will not understand one another's speech (Genesis 11:7).

The Prophet Isaiah recorded God saying: "Then I heard the voice of the Lord, saying, whom shall I send, and who will go for US?" Then I said, "Here am I. Send me" (Isaiah 6:8).

The Clearest Old Testament Statement is from the Prophet Isaiah. Come near me and listen to this: "From the first announcement I have not spoken in secret; at the time it happens, I am there." And now the Sovereign Lord has sent me, with his Spirit. This is what the Lord says "I am the Lord your God, who teaches you what is best for you, who directs you in the way you should go" (Isaiah 48:16, 17).

In verse sixteen, God the Son is speaking. He identifies the Father (the Sovereign Lord) and His Spirit as having sent Him. In the next verse, the Son is clearly spoken of as the Lord. Consequently these verses identify three distinct Persons who are God without denying the fact there is only one God. Each member of the Trinity is mentioned in the Old Testament.

God the Father

For you are our father, though Abraham does not know us and Israel does not acknowledge us; you, O Lord, are our father; our Redeemer from of old is your name (Isaiah 63: 16).

Malachi wrote: "Have we not all one father? Has not one God created us? Why then are we faithless to one another, profaning the covenant of our ancestors"? (Malachi 2:10).

God the Son

In the Second Psalm we read: "I have set my king on Zion, my holy hill. I will tell of the decree of the Lord: He said to me, "You are my Son; today I have begotten you" (Psalm 2:6, 7).

Psalm 2: 12 says: "Kiss the Son, lest he be angry, and you perish in the way, when his wrath is kindled but a little. Blessed are all those who put their trust in him".

Proverbs says: "Who has gone up to heaven and come down? Who has gathered up the wind in the hollow of his hands? Who has wrapped up the waters in his cloak? Who has established all the ends of the earth? What is his name, and the name of his son? Tell me if you know" (Proverbs 30:4).

Isaiah wrote: "For to us a child is born, to us a son is given, and the government will be on his shoulders. And he will be called Wonderful Counselor, Mighty God, Everlasting Father, Prince of Peace" (Isaiah 9: 6).

God the Holy Spirit

The Holy Spirit, or the "Spirit of the Lord," is also mentioned in the Old Testament. In the Book of Genesis we read: Now the earth was formless and empty, darkness was over the surface of the deep, and the Spirit of God was hovering over the waters (Genesis 1:2).

The Prophet Isaiah recorded the following: The Spirit of the Lord will rest on him - the Spirit of wisdom and of understanding, the Spirit of counsel and of power, the Spirit of knowledge and of the fear of the Lord - and he will delight in the fear of the Lord. He will not judge by what he sees with his eyes, or decide by what he hears with his ears (Isaiah 11:2,3).

Isaiah also wrote: The Spirit of the Sovereign Lord is on me, because the Lord has anointed me to preach good news to the poor. He has sent me to bind up the brokenhearted, to proclaim freedom for the captives and release from darkness for the prisoners (Isaiah 61: 1).

Isaiah 63: 10 says: "Yet they rebelled and grieved his Holy Spirit. So he turned and became their enemy and he himself fought against them".

The Spirit of God is distinguished from the Lord in the account leading up to the Flood. Then the Lord said, "My spirit shall not abide in mortals forever, for they are flesh; their days shall be one hundred twenty years" (Genesis 6:3).

God is Transcendent

God's transcendence refers to His distance, His separation from all else. He is infinitely exalted above all creation. According to Thomas Trevethan, as quoted by Muehlenberg (2020):

> God is other and sets apart from everything else that he is in a class by himself. God is not just quantitatively greater than us, but qualitatively different in his greatness. He is transcendent, infinitely above or beyond us. The true God is distinct, set apart, from all that he has made as the only truly self-sufficient Being. All his creatures depend on him; he alone exists from within himself.[87]

He goes on to postulate thus: "And the true God is distinct, set apart, from all that is evil. His moral perfection is absolute. His character as expressed in his will forms the absolute standard of moral excellence. God is holy; the absolute point of reference for all that exists and is good. Across the board he is to be contrasted with his creatures. At heart he is a glowing-white center of absolute purity."[88] Human language lacks the accuracy and concreteness to describe the transcendence nature of God.

God is not like his human creatures. He is sovereign and infinite; His creatures are not. He is perfect and pure and we are not. He is separate from us and independent from us. He does not need us but we need him. We are fully and always dependent on him. His transcendence, as noted, has a moral dimension: He is majestic, perfectly good, holy and pure. No

---

[87]Bill Muehlenberg's Commentary on Issues of the day in CultureWatch. Retrieved 6th March, 2020

evil can be allowed in his presence. He is implacable and utterly opposed to all that is evil and sinful. God and evil cannot coexist.[89]

The Prophet Isaiah 55:8-9 says, "For my thoughts are not your thoughts, neither are your ways my ways," declares the Lord. As the heavens are higher than the earth, so are my ways higher than your ways and my thoughts than your thoughts.

Psalm 113:5-6 – Who is like the Lord our God, the One who sits enthroned on high, who stoops down to look on the heavens and the earth? John 8:23 – You are from below, I am from above; you are of this world, I am not of this world.

According to Zemek, Psalm 113 provides a natural theological entrance into two corollary truths about God, His transcendence and His immanence'. Here, the Psalmist says: [*a*]ll men to let the praise of God resound all the world over and motivates the appeal with the declaration that this incomparable God, transcending the heavens in glory, is the Sovereign of the world who controls the affairs of men below from his throne.[90]

God is Immanent

God is not just transcendent; he is also immanent, He is very near. God is wholly present with and active in the created order. God is near us, present with us, active on earth and involved in the dynamics of our world. He is present and active in nature, in history, in our lives. He acts in this world and dwells with his creatures.

God sent His Son to the world in order to have him well physically in his created cosmos. Jesus became one of us. He took human nature to be what humanity is except sin. He

---

[88]Ibid

[89]Ibid

[90]Zemek, G.J., 1990, 'Grandeur and Grace: God's transcendence and immanence in Psalms 113', *The Masters Seminary Journal* 1(2), 129–148.

became God that dwells among humanity, not a God who is far, aloof, and unconcerned with his creatures. He actually became what we are so that we become like him.

From the very beginning of Scripture we read about God's immanence: "Then the man and his wife heard the sound of the Lord God as he was walking in the garden in the cool of the day, and they hid from the Lord God among the trees of the garden" (Genesis 3:8).

The incarnation is the greatest expression of this truth: John 1:14 – The Word became flesh and made his dwelling among us. We have seen His glory, the glory of the One and Only, who came from the Father, full of grace and truth.

God is personally immanent within humankind in the person of his only begotten Son, as the new Adam for the sake of our redemption. As Torrance (2008) puts it:

> within this human-inhuman existence of Adam, Jesus Christ comes as the Son of God, the Son of man as Jesus calls himself, to live out a truly obedient and filial, that is a truly human life, in perfect and unbroken union with God the Father ... In all of that Jesus Christ is the last Adam, the one who...brings to an end the bondage of Adam's sin, breaks its power and opens up a new and living way to God.[91]

To buttress this further, Philippians 2:6 relevantly says that Christ, "although He existed in the form of God, did not regard equality with God a thing to be grasped, but emptied Himself, taking the form of a servant, and being made in the likeness of men." Ephesians 4:6 states that "there is one God and Father of all, who is over all and through all and in all." This is the quotation Muslims use to reject the Trinitarian scope of God. In their understanding, God cannot be pluralised.

---

[91]Torrance, T.F., (2008). Incarnation: The person and life of Christ, IVP Academic, Downers Grove

In contrast, Pantheism[92] denies God's transcendence and Deism[93] also denies God's immanence. Christianity affirms both, especially as expressed in the incarnation. The Biblical texts stressing both his immanence and transcendence are many. Here are just a few:

Deuteronomy 4:39 says "Acknowledge and take to heart this day that the Lord is God in heaven above and on the earth below. There is no other". Isaiah 57:15 "For this is what the high and lofty One says – he who lives forever, whose name is holy: "I live in a high and holy place, but also with him who is contrite and lowly in spirit, to revive the spirit of the lowly and to revive the heart of the contrite".

Jeremiah 23:23-24 "Am I only a God nearby," declares the Lord, "and not a God far away? Can anyone hide in secret places so that I cannot see him?" declares the Lord. "Do not I fill heaven and earth?" declares the Lord.

Luke 11:2 "Our father (immanence) who art in heaven (transcendence)"...Paul puts it in his speech to the Athenians in Acts 17:24-28: "The God who made the world and all things in it, since He is Lord of heaven and earth, does not dwell in temples made with hands; neither is He served by human hands, as though He needed anything, since He Himself gives to all life and breath and all things; and He made from one, every nation of mankind to live on all the face of the earth, having determined their appointed times, and the boundaries of their habitation, that they should seek God, if perhaps they might grope for Him and find Him, though He is not far from each one of us; for in Him we live and move and exist."

When it comes to God's transcendence, the Scripture uses metaphors of farness or distance, and speaks about him as

---

[92]the belief that reality is identical with divinity, or that all-things compose an all-encompassing

[93]A philosophical belief that posits that God exists and is ultimately responsible for the creation of the universe, but does not interfere directly with the created world.

creator, king, judge, warrior, master, and so on. When discussing divine immanence, the Scripture uses metaphors of nearness or closeness, and speaks about Him as bridegroom, father, shepherd, husband, lover, and so on. God who is both near and far as C.S. Lewis puts it in *The Problem of Pain*, "God is both further from us, and nearer to us, than any other being."

God is Omniscient

The omniscience of God is the norm that God is all-knowing; that He encompasses all knowledge of the universe past, present, and future. It is the state of having full knowledge of everything that is. Some modern Christian theologians argue that God's omniscience is inherent rather than total, and that God chooses to limit his omniscience in order to preserve the freewill and dignity of His creatures.[94]

Hence, for God to be supreme over His creation, whether visible or invisible, He has to be all-knowing. Psalm 147: 4-5 says, "He determines the number of the stars and calls them each by name. Great is our Lord and mighty in power; his understanding has no limit."

Given His limitlessness, God discerns everything that is in the world and beyond (1John 3:20). He knows not only the minutest details of our lives but of everything around us, for He mentions even knowing when a sparrow falls or when we lose a single hair (Matthew 10:29-30). God does not only identify everything that will occur until the end of time (Isaiah 46:9-10), but also knows our very thoughts, even before we speak out (Psalm 139:4). He knows our innermost thoughts and our hearts from afar; He also knew us in the womb (Psalm 139:1-3, 15-16). "For you, you only, know the hearts of all the children of mankind" (1Kings 8:39).

The omniscience of God is demonstrated in His knowledge of his creatures and plan for their lives even before they came to be. He knows us better than we know ourselves. Matthew 10:30

---

[94]Polkinghorne, J. (1998). Science and Theology SPCK/Fortress Press.

says that even the hairs on our head are numbered. No matter how cautious we are in keeping our secrets from others, they are all known to God. Proverbs 15:3 articulates that: “The eyes of the Lord are everywhere, keeping watch on the wicked and the good.” God understands how we feel when we are going through stiff times because He knows our thoughts and feelings. The God who knows every star by name knows each of us personally and loves us indefinitely. “For the Lord searches every heart and understands every desire and every thought” (1Chronicles 28:9).

The omniscience of God is reflected in the Acts of the Apostles 1: 24 when the Apostles had their very first prayer to God: “Lord, you know everyone's heart,” this infers Jesus' omniscience, which is necessary if He is to be able to receive petitions and intercede at God's right hand. In the Gospel, the omniscience God knew the thoughts of his audience (Matthew 9:4; 12:25; Mark 2:6-8; Luke 6:8). He knew about people's lives before He had even met them. To the woman at the well Jesus said, “The fact is you have had five husbands, and the man you now have is not your husband” (John 4:18). He also tells His disciples that their friend Lazarus was dead, although He was over 25 miles away from Lazarus's home (John 11:11-15). He advised the disciples to go and make preparation for the Lord's Supper, describing the person they were to meet and follow (Mark 14:13-15). He knew Nathanael before ever meeting him, for He knew his heart (John 1:47-48).

A conundrum is presented when Jesus asked questions. To make enquiry could, in the first instance, be an indication of lack of knowledge, it could also be for the one asked to provide an answer by himself. In the case of Jesus, his questions were not absence of knowledge but for the benefit of His audience. However, there is another facet regarding His omniscience that comes from the limitations of the human nature which He, as Son of God, assumed. We read that as a man He “grew in wisdom and stature” (Luke 2:52) and that He learned “obedience through suffering” (Hebrew 5:8). We also read that He did not know when the world would be brought to an end

(Matthew 24:34-36). We, therefore, have to ask, why would the Son not know this, if He knew everything else? Rather than regarding this as just a human limitation, we should regard it as a controlled lack of knowledge. This was a self-willed act of humility in order to share fully in our nature (Philipians 2:6-11; Hebrew 2:17) and to be the Second Adam.

God of Mercy

Having seen the omniscience of God, it is necessary to understand that it also expressed in His mercy. Understanding mercy is often difficult for people because mercy itself, as an attribute of God, is easy to receive than to give. Like other attributes, mercy has no regard for or conditions toward the person, it is an attribute of God within and of Himself, with no foundation or regard for the creature or the recipient. "Mercy" should not be seen as only a "feeling" or emotion that God has and is surely not a temporary mood, but it is also a power, an infinite and inexhaustible energy. We cannot gauge God's mercy toward us, much less toward Himself, so we confine our thoughts to His mercy toward His creation and His creatures, particularly humankind. Norman writes:

> Mercy flows from God's attribute of goodness (or love) as grounded in His infinity and immutability. Since God is unlimited and unchangeable, then, given that He is good, He must be infinitely and unchangeably good. Since mercy flows from God's goodness, and since God is infinite, it follows that God is infinitely and unchangeably merciful. It is of His very nature to show mercy; He cannot not be merciful. As God is a necessary Being, even so He must of necessity be merciful. Were He not merciful, He would not be *essentially* good or loving. God is not *arbitrarily* merciful.[95]

The infinite mercy of God most times makes humankind to confuse it with grace. While similar in meaning, they are two different ideas. Mercy is God not punishing us as our sins

---

[95]Norman, G. *Systematic Theology*, 389.

deserve and not forgetting He is a just. Grace is God blessing us despite the fact that we don't deserve it. It is unmerited favour.

Since we are all sinners (Romans 3:23), we deserve death (Romans 6:23), so every day we live is an act of mercy from God. We deserve nothing from God. Any good thing that comes into our life is a result of the grace of God (Ephesians 2:5).

We receive mercy from God but some people find it cumbersome to be merciful. God, however, is merciful to even the worst offenders, sinners, and law-breakers. This means that even though He knows of our guilt, He doesn't always issue the punishment deserved. This is elaborated in Romans 3:23-24 where it says "...all have sinned and fall short of the glory of God, and are justified freely by his grace through the redemption that came by Christ Jesus."

We are all sinners and do not meet the standards of righteousness that God intends us to have. However, through His mercy and grace, He provides a way for our sins to be forgiven through our acceptance of Christ Jesus—even though we do not deserve it. Coupled with grace (being given God's free gift of forgiveness though we've done nothing to deserve it), mercy is shown because He loves us and only asks that we accept His Son by faith.

In a similar line, Micah 6: 8 says "He has showed you, O man, what is good. And what does the Lord require of you? To act justly, and to love mercy and to walk humbly with your God." These are words to all of humankind. He has shown us what isgood and answers what is required of us. Micah asks God in 7:8, "Who is a God like you, who pardons sin and forgives the transgression of the remnant of his inheritance? You do not stay angry forever but delight to show mercy."

The mercy of God is shown in the Bible. For instance, in Genesis 37 through 45 the story of Joseph, son of Jacob is found. God's mercy toward Joseph's brothers for their betrayal is certainly evident in this story. Other illustrations are found throughout the prayers of King David in the Psalms. God's mercy is endless and is found throughout the ages to the present.

Paul puts it well in Ephesians 2:4-10"But because of his great love for us, God, who is rich in mercy, made us alive with Christ even when we were dead in transgressions, it is by grace we are saved. And God raised us with Christ and seated us with him in the heavenly realms in Christ Jesus, in order that in the coming ages he might show the incomparable riches of his grace, expressed in his kindness to us in Christ Jesus. For it is by grace you have been saved, through faith, and this not from yourselves, it is the gift of God, not by works, so that no one can boast. For we are God's workmanship, created in Christ Jesus to do good works, which God prepared in advance for us to do."

Monotheism in Islam

The belief in one God, is one of the most important and foundational concepts in Islam. Muslims believe in one God who created the universe and has power over everything within it. He is unique and exalted above everything He created, and His greatness cannot be compared to His creation. He is the only one deserving of any worship and the ultimate purpose of all creation is to submit to Him.

The name of God in Islam is *Allah*, an Arabic word which means he is indivisible, absolute, all-powerful; and all-knowing ruler of the universe, and the creator of everything in existence within the universe. In Islam God is strictly singular *(tawhid)*: unique (*wāḥid*), inherently One (*aḥad*)[96] God is also all-merciful and omnipotent.[97] According to Islamic traditions and the Quran, "No vision can grasp him, but His grasp is over all vision: He is above all comprehension, yet is acquainted with all things." (Quran 6:103). According to *The Noble Quran* 112, "He is God, (who is) One. God, the Eternal Refuge. He neither begets nor is born, nor is there to Him any equivalent."

---

[96]John L. E. (1998). Islam: The Straight Path, Oxford University Press, p.88

[97]Allah."Encyclopedia Britannica. 2007.

Islam, given the respect and the awesomeness it attaches to God, has 99 known names for God regarded by Muslims as "The best names" of Him who neither begets nor is born, each of which evokes a distinct attribute of God.[98] All these names refer to *Allah*, the supreme and all-comprehensive God. Among the 99 names of God, the most familiar and frequent are "the Compassionate" (*Ar-Raḥmān*) and "the Merciful" (*Ar-Raḥīm*).[99]

These names are traditionally computed as 99 in number to which *al-ism al-aẓam* is added as the maximum name, the Supreme or Highest Name of *Allāh*. The *locus classicus* for listing the Divine Names in the literature of Qurānic commentary is 17: 110 "Call upon Allah, or call upon The Merciful; whichever you call upon, to *Allah* belong the most beautiful Names," and also 59:22-24which includes a cluster of more than a dozen Divine epithets."[100]

The Oneness of God (Tawhid)

As a strictly monotheistic religion, Islam's most fundamental concept of God is his Oneness, affirming that God is one and incomparable (*wāḥid*). The basic creed of Islam, the Shahada (recited under oath to enter the religion), is "I testify there is no god other than *Allah*." The veneration or worship of anyone or anything other than God (*shirk*) is the prime sin in Islam. The entirety of the Islamic teaching rests on the principle of Tawhid.[101] The religion of Islam is based on one core belief, that there is no god worthy of worship but *Allah*. When a person embraces Islam or a Muslim wants to renew or confirm his or her faith, they profess their belief that there is no god worthy of worship but Allah and that Muhammad is His final messenger. *Ashadu an la il illa Allah wa Ashadu anna Muhammadan Rasulullah*, Saying these words, the Testimony of Faith is the

---

[98] *Bentley, D. (1999). The 99 Beautiful Names for God for All the People of the Book. William Carey Library.*

[99] *Allah*: Encyclopedia of the Modern Middle East and North Africa.

[100] Böwering, Gerhard. "God and God Attributes". Encyclopedia of the Qur'ān.

[101] Tariq Ramadan, 2005, p.203.

first of five pillars or foundations of the religion of Islam. Belief in God is the first of five pillars of faith.

Quran 6:101-103 says "He is the Originator of the heavens and the earth. How can He have children when He has no wife? He created all things and He is the All-Knower of everything. Such is Allah, your Lord! *La ilahaillaHuwa* (none has the right to be worshipped but He), the Creator of all things. So worship Him (Alone), and He is the Trustee, Disposer of affairs, Guardian, over all things. No vision can grasp Him, but His Grasp is over all vision. He is the Most Subtle and Courteous, Well Acquainted with all things."

God as the Creator

God is not only limited to oneness but we must note that *Allah* in His physical and spiritual sense is one. He (*Allah*) is also understood and held as the creator, which is an attribute that is *al-Haliqu*-the creator of the universe and all the creatures in it. Surah (*Fatir*)-35:1 says *that* (All) praise is (due) to *Allah*, Creator of the heavens and the earth, (who) made the angels messengers having wings, two or three or four. He increases in creation what He wills. Indeed, Allah is over all things competent.

It is most relevant to again quote *Al Mu'minun-23:12* where the emphasis is on the act of creation. Hestates "We created man from an extract of clay. Then We made him as a drop in a place of settlement; firmly fixed (*Uterus of woman*). Then We made the drop into an alaqah (leech-like suspended blood clot), then We made the alaqah into a mudghah (chewed substances, little lump of flesh), then We made out of that mudghah bones, then We clothed the bones with flesh, and then We brought it forth as another creation. So blessed be Allah, the Best of creators." *Surah 4:1"*And God said: 'O Mankind! Be dutiful to your Lord, Who created you from a single person (Adam) and from Him (Adam) He created his wife (Eve), and from them both He created many men and women."['Iesa(Jesus) said]: "And verily Allah (God) is my Lord and your Lord. So worship Him (Alone). That is the Straight Path. (Allah's Religion of Islamic

Monotheism which He did ordain for all of His Prophets)." [Tafsir At-Tabari]. *Quran, Surah Maryam (Mary) 19:36.*

God of Mercy

God the Most Compassionate is the common name used by adherents of Islam. The most frequently used names in the primary sources are *Al-Rahman*, meaning "Most Compassionate" and *Al-Rahim*, meaning "Most Merciful".[102]The former compasses the whole creation, therefore, applies to God's mercy that gives every necessary condition to make life possible. The latter applies to God's mercy that gives favor for good deeds. Thus, *Al-Rahman* includes both the believers and the unbelievers, but *Al-Rahim* the believers.[103] Also, the word Rahman comes from the word Rahm which means the womb of the mother. It is a comparison between God's mercy to the mercy of a mother with her child.[104]

God's mercy takes many forms from the Quran *"and My Mercy embraces all things." [7:156]* this is shown by a narrative from Abu Hurairah. He said: "Allah has one hundred parts of mercy, of which He sent down one between the jinn, mankind, the animals and the insects, by means of which they are compassionate and merciful to one another, and by means of which wild animals are kind to their offspring. And Allah has kept back ninety-nine parts of mercy with which to be merciful to His slaves of the Day of Resurrection.[105] Also, God's mercy according to Islamic theology is what gets a person into paradise. According to Hadith in Shahih Al Bukhari "No one's deeds will ever admit him to Paradise." They said, "Not even you, O Messenger of Allah?" He said, "No, not even me, unless Allah showers me with His Mercy. So try to be near to perfection. And no one should wish for death; he is either doing

---

[102] Bentley, D. (1999). Op. Cit.

[103] Ayoub, M. (1984). The Qur'an and Its Interpreters , Volume 1Suny Press.

[104] Nouman Ali Khan.Lessons From Surah Ar Rahman,Retrieved 24/07/2018

[105] "My Mercy Prevails Over My Wrath" in https:// www.onislam.net. Retrieved 24/07/2018

good so he will do more of that, or he is doing wrong so he may repent."[106] Muhammad admits here that he will not be in paradise unless Allah showers him with his mercy.

God is Omniscient

God is not only one or creator but also has absolute knowledge of everything that is. God is described as being fully aware of everything that happens in the Universe, including private thoughts and feelings; nothing can be hidden from God who created all. "Say: Do you instruct Allah about your religion? But Allah knows all that is in the heavens and on the earth; Allah is knowing of all things" Holy Qur'an (49:16).

The Holy Qur'an 10:6 says, "And, (O Muhammad), you are not (engaged) in any matter or recite any of the Qur'an and you (people) do not do any deed except that We are witness over you when you are involved in it. And not absent from your Lord is any (part) of an atom's weight within the earth or within the heaven or (anything) smaller than that or greater but that it is in a clear register."

And indeed We have created man, and We know what his ownself whispers to him. And We are nearer to him than his jugular vein. *Quran, Sura Qaf: 50:16*

The omniscience of *Allah* shown in Qur'an 96:1-5 where it says: "Read! In the name of your Lord Who created. Created man of a clot. Read! And your Lord is the Most Bountiful, who taught man what he knew not..."We understand that scientists, engineers and designers who make airplanes, televisions, and cars, and doctors with medical knowledge, have gained and learned their subjects through schools, books and research. However, their vast knowledge is limited and they are not able to know everything or even have in-depth understanding in several fields.[107]

---

[106] "The Mercy of Allah Towards His slaves" in https://islamqa.info".Retrieved 24/07/2018.

[107] Islamic-doctrines-simplified in https://www.al-islam.org/ /allah-omniscient. Retrieved 24/07/2018

An engineer, who makes airplanes, is not familiar with the medical sciences, and eye-specialists have no knowledge of curing stomach sickness or heart complaints. It should also be noted that scientists and doctors depend upon tests and experiments before an invention can be developed, or a patient diagnosed. Their knowledge is based upon what has previously been learnt from higher knowledge that can come only from Allah.[108]

Allah the Omniscient knows everything in the heavens, what is on the earth and what is in the depths of seas. He knows the unknown and sees the unseen, what will happen tomorrow, after tomorrow and in the distant future, because He is the Creator of man and all creatures altogether. He knows what is known, what will be known and what never will be known by man because He created them, knowing everything in them, like an engineer who knows the machine which he himself made.[109] Nothing was, nothing is and nothing will be that is not known by the Creator of all creatures.

God is Transcendent and Immanent

Among the names and attributes of God are "Transcendent", "Superior" and "Exalted". The Creator Who provides for and takes care of this great universe should be "Transcendent", "Superior" and "Exalted". In Islam God is designated as both transcendent and immanent. While on the one hand it is said, "like Him there is naught" on the other hand the Quran says "We are nearer to him, than the jugular vein". In the sense of being Omni-present, God is immanent and also thought to be known indirectly by his creation.[110]

Allah is transcendent because "He is God, the One and Only God, the Eternal, Absolute; He begetteth not, nor is He begotten; And there is none like unto Him." (Sura 112:1-4). He

---

[108] Ibid.

[109] Ibid.

[110] Copleston, F. (2003). Religion and The One: Philosophies East and West A&C Black, page 96.

is Allah, other than whom there is no deity, the Sovereign, the Pure, the Perfection, the Bestower of Faith, the Overseer, the Exalted in Might, the Transcendent, and the Superior. Exalted is Allah above whatever they associate with Him (Al Hashr 59 :23).

The Qur'an confirms that transcendence and superiority belong to God in heaven and earth. It reads:Then, to *Allah* belongs (all) praise, Lord of the heavens and Lord of the earth, Lord of the worlds. And to Him belongs (all) superiority within the heavens and the earth, and He is the Exalted in Might, the Wise (Al Jathiyah 45:36-37).

CHAPTER THREE
SACREDNESS OF LIFE

"

How is it that we can presume the authority to take a life when that life has no say in the taking? And as I ponder that, I've come to think that it's less about taking the authority and more about the fact that somewhere along the way we've lost our respect for life. And if that's truly the case, then what else are we killing?"

- Craig D. Lounsbrough

The Abrahamic religions believe in the sacredness of life. Life is from God and a special gift, a blessing, and has dignity attached to it. Therefore, only God has the right to strip a person of this gift. There is the tendency to think that our lives are ours and we can handle them the way we so wish. Certainly, we have freedom to do so. However, we must not take undue advantage of our freedom to waste our lives or the lives of others. Judaism, Christianity and Islam are very vocal in anti-abortion, anti-euthanasia, and anti-war movements as they believe unjust killing is morally wrong and should be avoided.

As we express our faith, the erroneous belief that taking other people's lives in the name of God is serving God must be avoided. There is no rational argument that could make one to shed blood in the name of God. Again, there could be some commands from some sacred books that justify killing in the name of religion. However, there are tremendous reasons and explanations which demonstrate that saving life in the name of God is more than killing in the name of religion.

In this chapter, we shall see when life starts and when life is considered to be human. At what point should abortion be allowed? We shall also see how life should be respected and honoured. We shall discuss the meaning of life and how some religions mull over life.

The Gift of Life in Judaism

The Jews (Judaism) have a firm believe that humans were made as part of God's creation and in God's image. Human life, therefore, should be valued and considered sacred and God-given. Jews believe that only God can give life, and only God should take it.

In Judaism, life is extremely precious and sacred. Matters of life in whatever form are given optimal attention because life itself is a gift from God (Deuteronomy 30:19). The Jewish Talmudic Law believes that the full title to life arises only at birth.

Given the origin of life, Judaism, therefore, forbids acts that result in tampering with life whether in "mercy killing" or any measure that grants the "right to end life." In Judaism, life, until the moment of natural death, is inestimably valuable not just to the body, but to the Jewish people and the world as a whole.

The *halacha* (the collective body of Jewish religious laws derived from the written and Oral Torah) puts great value on human life, and views every human life as having infinite worth.[111] However, the fetus is seen as a "pre-human" life rather than a full life. Only at birth are full rights given to the fetus.[112] Although a fetus is not equal to a full human life, the

---

[111] Rosner F. Medicine and Jewish law. Northvale, NJ: Jason Aronson Inc; 1990. [Google Scholar]

[112] Halperin M, Fink D, Glick S. Jewish medical ethics.Vol. 2. Jerusalem: Schlesinger Institute for Medical-Halachic Research; 2006. [Google Scholar]

halacha still endows this potential life with certain rights and it is considered generally inviolable.

Since the fetus is given this status, it follows that abortion in the *halachic* view is prohibited, especially when the fetus has reached the human level. Different sources give several reasons on this teaching, but the ruling is largely based on the verse: "Whosoever sheddeth the blood of man in man, his blood shall be shed" (Genesis 9:6). Here, "man in man," is understood to be a fetus, and feticide is equated with murder.[113]

Murder is a crime that many religions frown at. There is, in Judaism, a strong objection to the procurement of abortion. It is neither permitted on the basis of genetic conditions nor other congenital deformity or for social reasons. Abortion has no grounds in Judaism whether on economic, career inconvenience or out of wedlock. However, some Rabbis are known to have given some window, especially in the early stages of gestation, within the first forty days, during which it is, according to one Talmudic statement, 'mere water'. The Babylonian Talmud Yevamot 69b states that: "the embryo is considered to be mere water until the fortieth day." Afterwards, it is considered subhuman until it is born.[114]

Most Jewish scholars admit that Jewish law permits abortion when the mother's life is in peril. This danger to the mother's life does not necessarily have to be definitive. It can be a probable threat to the mother's life.[115] This permission is based on an interpretation of the *halachic* term *rodef*, meaning 'pursuer'. This concept allows someone to kill a thief that is breaking into one's house, because one may assume that the

---

[113] Rosner F. Medicine and Jewish law.

[114] The beginning of Human Life: Status of embryo. Perspectives in Halakha (Jewish Religious Law) in https://www.ncbi.nlm.nih.gov/pmc/articles/PMC2582082/

[115] Halperin M, Fink D, Glick S. Jewish medical ethics.

thief is armed and may kill him or her. The fetus I,s thus, seen as a “pursuer,” which is threatening the mother's life. This threat must be stopped, even if it means killing the pursuer.[116]

This formulation of the attitude towards abortion in the classic sources of Jewish law implies:

1. That the only indication considered for abortion is a hazard to the mother's life;
2. That, otherwise, the destruction of an unborn child is a grave offence, although not murder; and
3. That it can be viewed that the fetus is granted some recognition of human life, but it does not equal that of the mother's, and can be sacrificed if her life is in danger.

The newborn child is not considered fully viable until it has survived thirty days following birth, as is stated in the Talmud: Rabban Simeon ben Gamliel said: Any human being who lives 30 days is not a *nephel* (abortus) because it is stated: 'And those that are to be redeemed of them from a month old shalt thou redeem (Numbers 18:16),' since prior to thirty days it is not certain that he will survive.”

Further support for the necessity of a 30-day postpartum viability period for adjudicating various Jewish legal matters pertaining to the newborn comes from Maimonides, who asserts:

> Whether one kills an adult or a day old child, a male or a female, he must be put to death if he kills deliberately... provided that the child is born after a full term pregnancy. But, if it is born before the end of nine months, it is regarded as an abortion until it has lived for thirty days, and if one kills it during these thirty days, one is not put to death on its account.

[116] Rosner F. Medicine and Jewish law.

Thus, although the newborn infant reaches the status of a person or *nefesh,* which it did not have prior to birth, it still does not enjoy all the legal rights of an adult until it has survived for thirty days postpartum. The death penalty is not imposed if one kills such a child before it has established its viability, but killing it is certainly prohibited because "one may not set aside one person's life for that of another."

Jewish law does not consider a fetus to be alive. The Torah, Exodus 21:22-23, recounts the story of two men who are fighting and injure a pregnant woman resulting in her subsequent miscarriage. The verse explains that if the only harm done is the miscarriage, then the perpetrator must pay a fine. However, if the pregnant person is gravely injured, the penalty shall be a life for a life as in other homicides. The common rabbinical interpretation of this verse is that the men did not commit murder and that the fetus is not a person. The primary concern is the well-being of the person who was injured.

Sacredness of Life in Christianity

Christianity teaches that human life is sacred and that the dignity of the human person is the foundation of a moral vision for society. This belief is taken to be the foundation of all the principles of the Catholic social teaching. Today, human life is under direct attack from abortion, euthanasia and other life threatening issues. The value of human life is being susceptible by cloning, embryonic stem cell research, and the use of the death penalty.[117]

Life is a unique gift to man. It"... is a characteristic that distinguishes physical entities that have biological processes, such as signaling and self-sustaining processes, from those that do not, either because such functions have ceased (they

[117] Principles of Catholic Social Teachings in https://catholiccharitiescamden.org/principles-of-catholic-social-teaching

have died), or because they never had such functions and are classified as inanimate. Various forms of life exist, such as plants, animals, fungi, protists, archaea, and bacteria. The criteria can at times be ambiguous and may or may not define viruses, viroids, or potential synthetic life as living."[118] Any life that comes to existence is permitted by God, and it is assumed to have a certain purpose.

Life is considered sacred because it comes from God. 'Sacred' means revered due to sanctity and is generally the state of being perceived by religious individuals as associated with divinity and considered worthy of spiritual respect or devotion; or inspiring awe or reverence among believers Wikipedia.[119] Non-religious individuals would simply acknowledge life as coming from God but may not necessarily understand how sacred or what makes life sacred.

In the spiritual realm, life is known to be a special gift from God to man and the right to life is deeply rooted in the Bible. God made man in His image and likeness and breathed into him his own life so that man's life becomes abundantly relevant to His (Genesis 2:7). This 'transfer' of life did not happen with the animals and the plants, but only with man. Man shares in the nature of God. "So God created man in his own image, in the image of God he created him; Male and female he created them" (Genesis 1:26-27).

The Old Testament is replete with stories of God's involvement in the affairs of mankind, and of His love for His creation. David in the Psalms repeatedly speaks of God's relationship with Man. The cradle of the Christian faith is that God so much loved humanity that He gave His only son as a ransom to save all people from death. Life, therefore, is remarkably precious in Christianity. This shows that

---

[118] Sacred in Wikipedia, Retrieved 22/07/18

[119] Ibid

humanity in some way is a reflection of God. In humans, something of God himself can be seen.

The sacredness or sanctity of life has always been a controversial issue in the moral and even political space. Pro-life movements have always had problems with some political organisations or countries that have debased the sanctity of life ranging from abortion, contraception, euthanasia, embryonic or stem-cell research and other life related issues. The stand of the pro-life movement stems from the strong respect for life as a sovereign gift from God.

> "Human life is sacred because from its beginning it involves the creative action of God and it remains forever in a special relationship with the Creator, who is its sole end. God alone is the Lord of life from its beginning until its end: no one can under any circumstance claim for himself the right directly to destroy an innocent human being" (*Donum Vitae*, 5).[120]

Respect for the sacredness of life from the womb originates from Christian Jewish roots. For the Jews, human life is authored by One God whose creative power produces the child in the mother's womb and brings it step-by-step to full life. The Old Testament revelation which the Church inherited and accepted, gives clear evidence that life in the womb is considered sacred.

Given the revelation of the Old and New Testaments, with special emphasis on the mystery of Incarnation, the Church has condemned in totality, the inhuman trivialities of life, especially on the practice of abortion and its relevant attendants. Several examples of Christian teaching from the first three hundred years of the Church include The *Didache* (*The Teachings of the Twelve Apostles*) (c. AD 80) which states that, "You shall not procure abortion. You shall not destroy the newborn child." The *Epistle of Barnabas* (AD 138)

---

[120] Donum Vitae, 5

also condemns abortion. Athenagoras (AD 177) in his *A Plea on Behalf of Christians* (a defense against paganism) emphasised that Christians consider as murderers those women who take medicines to procure an abortion. He condemns the killer of children, including those still living in their mothers' wombs, "where they are already the object of the care of divine providence." Tertullian (AD 197) in his *Apologeticum* asserts, "To prevent birth is anticipated murder; it makes little difference whether one destroys a life already born or does away with it in its nascent stage. The one who will be man is already one." In the year 300, the Council of Elvira, a local Church council in Spain, also passed specific legislation condemning abortion (Canon 63).

After the endorsement of Christianity in AD 313, the denunciation of abortion remained. St. Basil, in a letter to Bishop Amphilochius (AD 374), clearly pronounces the Church's teaching thus: "A woman who has deliberately destroyed a fetus must pay the penalty for murder" and "Those also who give drugs causing abortions are murderers themselves, as well as those who receive the poison which kills the fetus."

While many other examples abound on the subject matter, the emphasis is that the Church from the beginning till date has unswervingly upheld the sanctity of the life of the unborn child and condemns in very strong terms the act of direct abortion. To oppose this teaching contradicts the revelation of Sacred Scripture and Christian tradition.

Among all the crimes which can be committed against life, procured abortion has characteristics making it particularly severe and deplorable. The Second Vatican Council defines abortion, together with infanticide, as an "unspeakable crime."[121] The texts of Sacred Scripture never address the

---

[121] *Gaudium et spes*, 51.

question of deliberate abortion and so do not directly and specifically condemn it. Scripture passages show such great respect for the human being in the mother's womb that they require as a logical consequence that God's commandment "You shall not kill" be extended to the unborn child as well... Christian Tradition as the Declaration issued by the Congregation for the Doctrine of the Faith points out so well is clear and unanimous, from the beginning up to our own day, in describing abortion as a particularly grave moral disorder.

Similarly, Paul VI declares that direct abortion, that is, abortion willed as an end or as a means, always constitutes a grave moral disorder, since it is the deliberate killing of an innocent human being. This doctrine is based upon the natural law and upon the written Word of God, is transmitted by the Church's Tradition and taught by the ordinary and universal Magisterium.[122]

The question on when abortion could be permitted is a disturbing phenomenon in morality. This is where the principle of double effect is frequently cited in relation to abortion. A medic who detests abortion may nevertheless remove the uterus or fallopian tube of a pregnant woman, knowing full well the procedure will cause the death of the embryo or fetus, in cases in which the woman is certain to die without the procedure (examples cited include aggressive uterine cancer and ectopic pregnancy). In these cases, the intended effect is to save the woman's life, not to terminate the pregnancy, and the death of the embryo or fetus is a side effect. The death of the fetus is an undesirable but unavoidable consequence.[123] The saving of the mother's life is intended and the dead of the fetus is unintended.

---

[122] Evangelium vitae, §§ 58, 61-62.

[123] McIntyre, Alison. "Doctrine of Double Effect".In Edward N. Zalta. Stanford Encyclopedia of Philosophy (Summer 2006 ed.. Retrieved 22/07/18.

Ectopic pregnancy is one of the uncommon cases where the conventional death of an embryo is permissible, since it is considered as an indirect abortion. This opinion was also supported by Pius XII in a 1953 address to the Italian Association of Urology on indirect abortion.

In line with the Thomistic Principle of Totality (removal of a pathological part to preserve the life of the person) and the Doctrine of Double Effect, the only moral action in an ectopic pregnancy where a woman's life is directly threatened is the removal of the tube containing the human embryo (salpingectomy). The death of the human embryo is unintended although foreseen.[124]

The embryo has life and the Church teaches that "human life must be respected and protected absolutely from the moment of conception. From the first moment of his existence, a human being must be recognized as having the rights of a person among which are the inviolable right of every innocent being to life."[125] This follows from the fact that probabilism may not be used where human life may be at stake.[126]

In the similar light, the Catholic Catechism teaches that the embryo must be treated from conception "as" (Latin: *tamquam,* "as if") a human person (CCC2274). *The New Catholic Encyclopedia* concludes: After a certain stage of intrauterine development it is perfectly evident that fetal life is fully human. Although some might speculate as to when that stage is reached, there is no way of arriving at this knowledge by any known criterion; and as long as it is probable that embryonic life is human from the first moment of its existence, the purposeful termination (is immoral).[127]

---

[124] ALL: The moral management of ectopic pregnancies.

[125] Catechism of the Catholic Church - IntraText"in www.vatican.va.

[126] The Tradition of Probabilism and the Moral Status of the Early Embryo".Theological Studies.

[127] New Catholic Encyclopedia, Abortion II, p.29, Col 1.

In order to give life its rightful place, the Magisterium has carefully avoided confusing "human being" with "human person", and avoids the conclusion that every embryonic human being is a person, which would raise the question of "ensoulment" and immoral destiny.[128]

With regards to this understanding, the alienable right to life of every innocent human being is a constitutive element of a civil society and its legislation. In other words, it is beholden upon society to legally protect the life of the unborn (CCC, part 3, section 2, chapter 2, article 5).[129] Human life is considered sacred and it starts at the point of conception. The deliberate destruction or tampering with the embryo, blastocyst, zygote or fetus as the case may be is unacceptable in Christian understanding. The Church, however, is not unaware of some conditions that could inadvertently lead to the 'destruction' of the embryo, blastocyst, zygote or fetus.

The Sacredness of Life in Islam

Adherents of Islam like other religions believe all life is created by *Allah*, and only *Allah* has the power to take life. Murder is explicitly forbidden by the Quran. The Muslim understanding ofabortion is formed by the Hadith[130] as well as by the opinions of legal and religious scholars and commentators. The Quran does not directly address intentional abortion, leaving greater discretion to the laws of individuals and countries. In Islam, the fetus is believed to become a living soul after four months of gestation (Sahih al Bukhari 4:54:430).

According to the report of Shaykh al-Uthaymin, the most acceptable legal position on abortion in Islam is that it is a

---

[128] ("The Wisdom of the Church Is in Her Silence, Too". National Catholic Register. Retrieved 22/07/18

[129] Ibid.

[130] The Record of the Words, Actions, and the Silent Approval, of the Islamic Prophet Muhammad.

prohibited act because of the Quranic injunction that states: Then we placed it in place of safety (womb) for a known period (determined by gestation) (Quran 77:20-21). Hence, it is prohibited and unlawful to abort the fetus. However, under clear necessity, according to other views, abortion could be committed even if the fetus has reached four months after life has been blown into the body.

As the Qur'an 6: 151 says, "Take not life which *Allah* has made sacred", it however, does not explicitly refer to abortion but offers guidance on related matters. Scholars accept that this guidance can properly be applied to abortion.

In relation to the understanding of abortion, Quran 5: 32 says that, "We ordained for the children of Israel that if anyone slew a person, unless it be for murder or for spreading mischief in the land, it would be as if he slew the whole of mankind. And if anyone saved a life, it would be as if he saved the life of a whole people."(Some form of interpretation may be needed here to know whether the statement was directed to the children of Israel or not).

Concerning taking of life in times of military engagement, the warriors are duty bound not to destroy civilian life. It is consequently unlawful to attack women and children, the elderly and the insane, the ill and the invalid and this include the blind, the lame, the crippled and the unconscious. The exempted categories also include the Priests and the Monks and those engaged in worship as well as farmers who occupy themselves with their work in the field provided that they are not involved in the conflict. The *hadith* contains detailed instructions on all of these and the Prophet has generally advised military commanders and soldiers in the battlefield to be fair, avoid excessive violence and incline toward peace.[131&132]

---

[131] Zuhayli, Al-Fiqh al-IslamiwaAdillatuh, VI, 421 ff.{/qluetip}

[132] The Dignity of Man - the Islamic Perspective, Ilmiah Publishers, Malaysia and the Islamic Foundation, UK, ©1999

In Quran 17:33 the sanctity of life is clearly upheld as the prophet says, "Do not take life which *Allah* has made sacred, except for just cause. And if anyone is slain wrongfully, we have given his heir authority (to demand qisas or to forgive): but let him not exceed bounds in the matter of taking life; for he is helped (by the Law). Muhammad al-Ghazali has quoted these *ayat* and drew the conclusion that "in respect of the sanctity of life and the prohibition of aggression against it, Muslims and non-Muslims are equal. Attack on the personal safety of non-Muslims invokes the same punishment in this world and the Hereafter."[133]

Consequently, the Quran makes it clear thus: "Come, I will rehearse what *Allah* hath (really) prohibited you from: Join not anything as equal with Him; be good to your parents; kill not your children on a plea of want; we provide sustenance for you and for them; come not nigh to shameful deeds. Whether open or secret; take not life, which *Allah* hath made sacred, except by way of justice and law: thus doth He command you, that ye may learn wisdom. (6:151).

This clearly indicates that Islam highly respects life. Murder is permissible only in extreme and 'just' circumstances. The Sanctity of life' is prioritised in Islam. Life is sacred and only God gives and should take it. The actual point by which life is substantially valued as human is, however, disputed in Islamic theology. Some scholars believe it is 120 days, others believe it is 40 days. Another opinion is when the baby voluntarily moves inside the womb.

There are some situations in Islam where abortion is permitted, and indeed recommended. Different Muslim schools of thought have different beliefs about abortion. However the main ones recognise that it is necessary at times, and nearly all accept that after 120 days, the only reason for

---

[133] qluetip title=[1]}Huquq al-Insan, p. 54{/qluetip

aborting a baby is if the life of the mother is in danger.[134] Abortion is regarded as a lesser evil in this case because:

- a the mother is the 'originator' of the fetus
- a the mother's life is well-established
- a the mother has with duties and responsibilities
- a the mother is part of a family
- a allowing the mother to die would also kill the fetus in most cases[135]

Another common situation about abortion is where the family aborts a baby under the pretext that it would not be able to provide for the baby properly – a pretext not accepted in Islam. The Quran specifies that abortion cannot be undertaken for fear of lack of resources to cater for the child as *Allah* will provide for the family. 'Kill not your offspring for fear of poverty; it is We who provide for them and for you. Surely, killing them is a great sin'(17:31). This ruling also extends to financial and social problems such as unplanned babies, and interference with the family or mother's plans for later life and career.

Abortion for the sake of the baby is a hotly debated discussion in Islam. Different scholars give different opinions about the actual abortion age, the process of choosing abortion for the sake of the baby is one which should be carefully considered. However, there is an almost unanimous decision that abortion after 120 days, for the baby's sake, is not permissible, unless the illness/defect in the baby would endanger the life of the mother.[136]

---

[134] Hedayat, K. M.; Shooshtarizadeh, P.; Raza, M. (2006)."Therapeutic abortion in Islam: Contemporary views of Muslim Shiite scholars and effect of recent Iranian legislation

[135] Sanctity of Life: Islamic Teaching on Abortion https://www.bbc.co.uk/religion/religions/islam/islamethics/abortion_1.shtml

[136] Bowen, Donna Lee (2003). "Chapter 3: Contemporary Muslim Ethics of Abortion". In Brockopp, Jonathan E (ed.). Islamic Ethics of Life: Abortion, War, and Euthanasia. Columbia, SC: University of South Carolina Press

Another opinion is if the defect is discovered early, and is thought by two competent medical specialists to have a physical and/or mental deformity that would greatly reduce the quality of the child's life, then an abortion before 120 days would be permissible. This opinion is agreed by several prominent Islamic scholars. A slightly more hard line view agrees with all those circumstances, bearing the child's actual deformity. These scholars take the opinion that the child's suffering must be untreatable and cause great suffering to him, in order to abort the child.[137]

Iran is politically and religiously governed by Ayatollah Ali Khameni, who, the Shi'ite branch of Muslims believe to be the current leader of all Muslims on earth. Recently, in Iran, he passed a 'fatwa' or Islamic law, to permit abortion for fetuses fewer than 10 weeks shown to have the thalassemia, a genetic blood disorder that causes severe anemia, and eventually leads to death.

Another Ayatollah of Iran, Yusuf Saanei issued another fatwa permitting abortion in the first three months for various reasons. Saanei claimed that abortion was generally forbidden in Islam, but claimed that; "But Islam is also a religion of compassion, and if there are serious problems, God sometimes doesn't require his creatures to practice his law. So under some conditions--such as parents' poverty or overpopulation--then abortion is allowed."[138]

While Yusuf Saanei's words apply to Shi'ite Muslims, they may be considered unacceptable to other branches of Islam. Therefore, the source that is heavily used is the decision of a resolution of the Islamic jurisprudence council of Mekkah Al

---

[137] "Sanctity of life". BBC News. 7 September 2009. Retrieved 29 March 2018.
[138] Grand Ayatollah Yusuf Saanei quoted in Los Angeles Times, December 29, 2000

Mukaramah (the Islamic World League,) who passed a fatwa in February 1990. Abortion was allowed in cases where the fetus was grossly malformed with untreatable severe condition proved by medical investigations and decided upon by a committee formed by competent trustworthy physicians, and provided that abortion is requested by the parents and the fetus is less than 120 days computed from moment of conception.[139]

Another situation in which abortion is considered in Islam is rape. This is a further controversial topic, where some people who would not normally allow abortion would make an exception. Some scholars claim that all life should be valued, whether the embryo is 'the result of fornication with relatives or non-relatives or valid marriage. In Sharia life has the same value in all cases.'[140]

However, a fatwa was issued to Bosnian women permitting abortion, when the Serbian army openly raped them.[141] A similar fatwa was passed in a similar terrible situation in Algeria.[142] Egypt, a prominent Islamic and Middle Eastern country (traditionally against abortion) issued a law that raped women were allowed abortions. This was a very controversial decision which stirred differences in opinion.[143] Abortion could only be permitted on certain conditions. Life is generally respected and considered sacred in Islam.

---

[139] Attributed, Mekkah Al Mukaramah, February 1990

[140] Sheikh M. A. Al-Salami, Third Symposium on Medical Jurisprudence.

[141] Abu-Hamad, Aziz (1995). "Rape as a Weapon of War".The Human Rights Watch Global Report on Women's Human Rights.

[142] C. Chelala "Algerian Abortion Controversy" https://www.ncbi.nlm.nih.gov/pubmed/9593424

[143] Hessini, Leila (May 2007). "Abortion and Islam: Policies and Practice in the Middle East and North Africa". Reproductive Health Matters.

CHAPTER FOUR

THE CONCEPT OF LOVE

"

Love says respect the other as an end unto himself or herself; never use the other as a means. Nobody is a means for you, everybody is an end. But then ambition will flop, and our whole educational system depends on ambitiousness, our politics depends on ambition, our religions depend on ambition.

- Rajneesh

Love is a natural instinct that does not necessarily require a religion to instruct its expression. Every human being has an innate crave that inspires him to appreciate something or someone. In like manner, we love without needing any qualification or attaining any status in life. Religion only reminds us of the need to practice love. The Abrahamic religions preach and profess love. They remind their adherents of the love of God, God's loves to his creatures and love among humanity.

In appreciating and understanding our different beliefs, the flow of love is a biding force that should not be interrupted or disturbed. Love must thrive across our religious lineages. We cannot claim to love God while we demonstrate hatred to adherents of other religions. If we truly love God and our religion, we must see God in the lives of people who do not believe in our God and our religion.

In this chapter, we shall see how the Abrahamic religions approach the concept of love; how love should be demonstrated and appreciated. Each religion epitomises love, yet there are slight differences in understanding and expressing love by the religions especially love towards members of other religions. The questions we need to ponder in this chapter among others are: should we hate 'them' because they are not 'us'? Should our different belief systems contradict the contents of love? If we truly believe that we are of the same 'source', then we must live and love as children of the same family. Our love must not only ignore boundaries but destroy them and scale across bridges of religious demarcations and neutralise hatred.

Love in Judaism

Love is defined in Hebrew as *ahavah,* which is rooted in the Aramaic word *hav* and literally translates as "give." For Rabbi Joseph Maroof, Judaism acknowledges that love, both of God and our fellow human beings, is a beautiful part of life that plays an important role in our emotional, spiritual and intellectual development.

In the Torah as found in Deuteronomy 6: 4–5, it is said: "Hear O Israel, the Lord is our God; the Lord is one. You shall love the Lord your God with all your heart, with all your soul, and with all your might." This command is taken by the *Mishnah* (the central text of the Jewish oral law) to refer to good deeds, willingness to sacrifice one's life rather than commit certain serious transgressions, willingness to sacrifice all one's possessions and being grateful to the Lord despite adversity.[144]

Love of God is highlighted as the highest incentive of action by Bahya ibn Pakuda, in "Ḥobot ha-Lebabot" (Jew. Encyc.ii.454). In *Duties of the Heart*, the Jewish philosopher maintaines that love of God is the ultimate goal and must be the aim of all virtues.[145] Bahya defines this love as the soul's longing for the creator and this is also made possible through

[144] Tractate Berachoth 9:5, Tractate Sanhedrin 74a.

[145] Cohn-Sherbok, Dan (2003). Judaism: History, Belief and Practice. New York: Psychology Press. p. 444.

the fear of God, which allows people to abstain from worldly desires.[146] It appears that fear is linked to love in the sense that it stems from the contemplation of God's power and greatness, which could result to emotional attachment seen in parts of the Psalm and elsewhere in the Bible.[147]

Once a religious person empties himself of the love for material things, he opens himself up to be filled with the love of God. These arguments led some observers to depict Bahya's perception of love towards the creator as more focused on the sentiment instead of putting emphasis on the rational or mystical aspects.[148] Love towards other people and even animals could fall within Bahya's framework when approached from his view that we cannot know God as He is in Himself and that it is only through his creatures that we can gain an apprehension of the Divine.[149] Love is to be directed to all creatures both animate and inanimate.

Given the importance of love, Maimonides writes that it should only be out of love for God, rather than fear of punishment or hope for reward that Jews should obey the law: "When man loves God with a love that is fitting he automatically carries out all the precepts of love."[150]

Hence, one of the core commandments of Judaism is "Love your neighbour as yourself" (Leviticus 19:18). This commandment stands at the centre of the central book in the Torah. But the word 'love' in the Torah is primarily an activist commandment: Love your neighbour and the stranger; love God. Even to love God, according to Talmud *Yoma* 26a, it

---

[146] Ibid.

[147] De *Lange, Nicholas (2002). An Introduction to Judaism. Cambridge: Cambridge University Press. pp. 198*

[148] *Ibid*

[149] *Cohn-Sherbock, Dan (1997). Fifty Key Jewish Thinkers. London: Routledge. p. 17.*

[150] Maimonides Yad Chapter 10, quoted in Jacobs 1973: 159

means we should behave divinely toward others, "making God beloved, through us."

Similarly, another significant commandment of love of neighbour is to "not stand idly by the blood of your neighbour" (Leviticus 19:16), which can be revealed in many forms. Some Jewish sources have emphasised the importance of self-sacrifice in regards to putting our needs second to another's. As 20th-century Jewish philosopher Martin Buber taught: "Love of the Creator and love of that which God has created, are finally one and the same." Love the stranger, whether documented or undocumented. Love your neighbour, regardless of whom they love in turn. And through these loving actions, you love God.

This commandment of love, with the preceding sentence, "Thou shall not avenge nor bear any grudge against the children of your people," may originally have referred, and has by some scholars (Stade, "Gesch. des Volkes Israel," i. 510a) been exclusively referred, to the Israelitish neighbour; but in verse 34 of the same chapter it is extended to "the stranger that dwells with you . . . and thou shall love him as yourself." In Job 31: 13–15 it is declared unjust to wrong the servant in his cause: "Did not he that made me in the womb make him? And did not one fashion us in the womb?"[151]

In Judaism, there is a mandate to love the non–Israelite who lives among Israelites, a reference to someone who does not worship the God of Israel or assimilate into the people of Israel. The verse says, "When a stranger resides with you in your land, you shall not wrong him... You shall love him as yourself, for you were strangers in the land of Egypt: I the Lord am your God" (Leviticus 20: 33, 34).

---

[151]Brotherly Love.in Jewish Encyclopedia.com. Retrieved 09.06.2020

However, if we return to K'doshim and carefully read both of these "love" verses in context, we see an altogether different meaning emerge. The few verses preceding "love your neighbour as yourself" tell us: do not render unfair decisions by favouring either the poor or the rich but judge fairly (Lev. 19: 15); do not deal basely with your countryman and do not profit from his blood (v. 16); do not hate him but rather reprove him (v. 17); do not take vengeance or bear a grudge against him (v. 18). These verses, which lead up to the concluding statement of this unit "Love him" define for the reader what "love" means when it is mandated for one's fellow man: in negative terms it means to refrain from treating him unfairly or abusing or exploiting him, and in positive terms it means to seek his welfare actively, to make sure that no one mistreats him. If this is how one Jew loves another Jew, then "love" makes even more sense when directed towards a stranger living among Jews.

The Torah says, do not wrong or oppress the stranger; instead, we should "love" him, meaning, to seek his welfare, to protect an outsider from abuse by insiders (Lev. 20: 34). The telltale phrase "because you were strangers in the Land of Egypt" means Jews should refrain from oppressing others because they remember what it is like to be taken advantage of. This clinches the argument. We were not seeking to have the ancient Egyptians love us, just not to treat us any differently from the way they treated each other.

Hillel[152] also uses the Biblical command when he responded to the heathen who requested him to tell him the Law while standing before him on one foot: "What is hateful to thee, thou shall not do unto thy neighbour. This is the whole of the Law, the rest is only commentary" (Shab. 31a). The negative form

[152]Hillel was a Jewish religious leader, sage and scholar associated with the development of the Mishnah and the Talmud and the founder of the House of Hillel school of tannaim.

was the accepted Targum interpretation of Lev. 19: 18, known alike to the author of Tobit 4:15 and to Philo, in the fragment preserved by Eusebius, "Preparatio Evangelica," viii. 7 to the Didache, i.1; Didascalia or Apostolic Constitutions, i.1, iii. 15. To include all men, Hillel used the term "beriot" (creatures as in Mark 16: 15; Rom. 8: 19).

Furthermore, Hillel's interpretation of "love your neighbour as yourself" to mean "what is hateful to you, do not do unto others," provides us with the simple meaning of the verse. Not that Hillel, as some say, was compromising on the requirement of actively loving other Jews, rather, he was explaining in this context of loving Jews and non-Jews. The Bible seeks to eradicate the exploitation and abuse of others, the kind we read about in Genesis 19 when the men of Sodom sought to molest the two out of town messengers. That is, the two verses about love, when not shorn of their context, are making the extraordinary statement that caring for self and family is not enough, and neither is avoiding abusing others. Jews must actively seek to eliminate injustice against Jews and non-Jews, wherever they see it.[153] This is as powerful social message as we also find in the Bible.

Hayyim Vital[154], the Kabbalist (school of thought in Jewish mysticism), in his "Sha'are edushah," i. 5 teaches that the law of love of the neighbour includes the non-Israelite as well as the Israelite.[155]

Similarly on love, the Rabbis of the Talmud interpreted the verses about loving non-Jews in an altogether different way.

---

[153]Judith Hauptman, E. Billi Ivry. Love all in http://www.jtsa.edu/love-for-all

[154]Hayyim ben Joseph Vital was a rabbi in Safed and the foremost disciple of Isaac Luria. He recorded much of his master's teachings. After Vital's death, his writings began to spread and led to a "powerful impact on various circles throughout the Jewish world."

[155]Brotherly Love in Jewish Encyclopedia.com. Retrieved on 09.06.2020

The Hebrew word "ger" meaning 'stranger' was co-opted by the rabbis to mean proselyte, someone who abandons his or her religion and adopts Judaism freely. This meaning of "ger" is standard to this very day. But, even after reinterpreting the word "ger" to mean "convert", the rabbis went on to apply the verse about loving the stranger to converts! That is, even though "ger" now meant something entirely different from what it used to, the rabbis maintained the biblical teachings on the subject of "ger." A convert may not be oppressed; his welfare must be sought.[156]

In the Hebrew Bible, *ahava* is used not only for God's love of his people and people's love of God (as in 'love God with all your heart', Deut. 6: 5) but also of the people's love of each other. 'Do not seek revenge or hold a grudge, but love your neighbour as yourself' (Lev. 19: 18). The imperative form of the verb (*ve-ahavta*), used elsewhere in the Pentateuch only with reference to man's love of God, is extended into a command to love one's *re a*, meaning 'other', 'companion', 'friend', or 'neighbour' as found in other translations. This is clear in Lev. 19: 34, "as you love yourself, love the foreigner (*ger*) residing in the land."

The most basic principle of Judaism is that, on a human level, we do not distinguish between those who are Jewish and those who live among Jews but are not Jewish. Furthermore, on a religious level, we do not distinguish between those who were born as Jews and those who chose to become Jews out of conviction. Every person who is born a Jew, every convert to Judaism, and every non–Jew who lives among us merits our active monitoring of his or her welfare and protection from discrimination and exploitation. This is the grand message of these two "love" verses of K'doshim.[157]

---

[156]Judith Hauptman, E. Billi Ivry. Love all in http://www.jtsa.edu/love-for-all

[157]Ibid

Explaining Lev. 19: 18 The Talmud puts it that even the criminal at the time of execution should be treated with tender love (Sanh. 45a). As Schechter in "J. Q. R." x. 11, shows, the expression "Ye have heard . . ." this is an inaccurate translation of the rabbinical formula, which is only a formal logical interrogation introducing the opposite view as the only correct one: "Ye might deduce from this verse that thou shalt love thy neighbour and hate thine enemy, but I say to you the only correct interpretation is, Love all men, even thine enemies."[158] This interpretation of the Talmud meets the desired love of the Jews. According to Ahad Ha-am, the Torah's phrasing of "thou shalt love thy neighbour as thyself" is negative because it creates a "perfect equilibrium, with no leaning either to your side or to your neighbour'"[159]

The 20th-Century Jewish theologian, Herberg (1951) argues that "justice" is at the heart of the Jewish notion of love, and the foundation for Jewish law:

> The ultimate criterion of justice, as of everything else in human life, is the divine imperative, the law of love.... Justice is the institutionalization of love in society.... This law of love requires that every man be treated as a Thou, a person, an end in himself, never merely as a thing or a means to another's end. When this demand is translated into laws and institutions under the conditions of human life in history, justice arises.[160]

In the Sermon on the Mount, Matthew, a Jewish Christian, presents his message in disparity with those that preceded him. In Matt 5:43-44 he says "You have heard that it has been said, you shall love your neighbour, and hate your enemy. But I say to you, Love your enemies, bless them that curse you, do

---

[158]Brotherly Love in Jewish Encyclopedia.com. Retrieved on 09.06.2020
[159]Ha-Am, Ahad.(1973). "Judaism and the Gospels."In Ten Essays on Zionism and Judaism, translated by Leon Simon, 241. New York: Arno Press,.
[160]Will Herberg(1951). Judaism and Modern Man, 148

good to them that hate you, and pray for them who despitefully use you, and persecute you". This according to some Jewish scholars was a misrepresentation of the Jewish teachings on love. This was a sectarian stratagem through which Jesus' teachings were presented as the perfection and fulfillment of a seeming flawed law from the Judaism. (A sectarian strategy that, in John, does take the form of a stress upon the love of one's 'friends' and brothers within the sectarian community, rather than one's 'enemies' outside of it: John 13: 34–5; 15: 9–13; 1 John 3: 14, 4: 12.)

Spinoza considered this law of hating the non-Jews as bad when he launched his revolutionary criticism of priestly political power in the *Theologico-Political Treatise* (= *TTP*) of 1670, he did so by suggesting that the basis of this power was in the bad laws of the Old Testament, bad because they instructed the Hebrews to love only themselves and hate all others outside themselves. Spinoza's choice of proof-text is striking: '[i]t was for this reason that they were told: "Love your neighbour and hate your enemy"' (*TTP* 216/iii.233, citing Matt. 5: 43).

The compilers of the Hebrew Bible had little trouble imagining God's love, whether for creation in general or for a particular person or people. In Deuteronomy 7: 7–8, 'the Lord did not set His heart upon you, nor choose you, because you were more numerous than any people, but because the Lord loved you, and because He would keep the oath which He swore unto your fathers.' Or as Prophet Hosea puts it, 'I led them with cords of human kindness, with ties of love. To them I was like one who lifts a little child to the cheek, and I bent down to feed them' (Hos. 11: 4). The Hebrew word for love used here is *ahava*, which roughly speaking includes the meaning of the Greek words *agape* ('true love' or love of God), *philía* (love between friends, love of wisdom), and *storgē* (familial love) (Moran 1963).[161]

[161]Moran, W. L. 1963.'The Ancient Near Eastern Background to the Love of God in Deuteronomy'.*Catholic Biblical Quarterly* 25: 77–87.

Classical commentators, of the Song of Songs Rabbah to the eleventh-century Rabbi Shlomo ben Yitzhak (Rashi), explained that Solomon known as the author of the Song of Songs wrote a love song in order to represent the love relationship between God and Israel in that Diasporic future. This song would remind Israel of her earlier marriage to God (cf. Hos. 2: 9), of her betrayal of that love (cf. Lev. 26: 40), and of her lover's ongoing suffering (cf. Isa. 63: 9), thereby recalling her to her divine spouse (cf. Hos. 2: 4).

Passionate love could represent the ideal relationship between God and people, but it could also show the infidelity of the people towards God. Solomon, for all his inspired knowledge of divine love, was led away from God by inappropriate erotic interests, as found in the Hebrew Bible in 1 Kgs 11).

The love of God towards his people is not directed only to the Jewish nation or community (Deut. 7: 7–8), 'The Lord is good to all and His tender mercies are over all his works' (Ps. 145: 9). God acts in the world for the benefit of all peoples, including Israel: 'Have not I brought up Israel out of the land of Egypt, and the Philistines from Caphtor, and the Syrians from Kir?' (Amos 9: 7).

The Concept of Love in Christianity

The word 'love' is used as expression of affection towards a person and could also express pleasure towards material things. To make it a little more complicated, the word "love" also expresses a human virtue that is based on compassion, affection and kindness. This is a state of being, that has nothing to do with something or someone outside oneself.

What is Love?

Several different Greek words are translated as "love" in the New Testament, and they have more specific meanings than the English word "love." Love is *Agapao* (verb) and *agape* (noun). It is the "Christian love" as found in the Bible. It means affection, benevolence, good-will, high esteem and concern for the welfare of the one loved. It is deliberate, purposeful love rather than emotional or impulsive love. Almost all of the New Testament references to love are *agapao* or *agape* in the original Greek language. Some Biblical translations sometimes translate *agape* as "charity," but charity in modern times has now taken on the meaning of assistance to the poor rather than benevolent love.

Another word for love is *Phileo* (verb). This means to love in an impulsive and emotional way. It is seldom used in the Bible. There is a play on words in John 21:15-17 where Jesus says to Peter, "Simon son of John, do you truly love (*agapao*) me?" Peter answers, "Yes, Lord, you know that I love (*phileo*) you." Also, *Philadelphia* is another word for love which is a related word meaning the love of brothers or sisters (example, Romans 12:10). It is often translated "brotherly love." It is important to have a look at the different types of love that there are. According to ancient Greek, there are seven different kinds of love namely:

Storge: natural affection, love shared among family members.

Philia: love for friends.

Eros: sexual and erotic kind of love.

Agape: unconditional love, or divine love

Ludus: playful love, childish love or flirting.

Pragma: long standing love. Love between married couple.

Philautia: love of self.

These seven kinds of love also mean different ways through which the individual expresses his or her feelings. The love of a mother towards her son is distinct from the love a man has for his wife; and every love has the capacity of transformation. There are different emotions for different people and situations. This could bring about misperception in demonstrating and communicating or expressing love because the same word "love" is used. The phrase "I love you" could be used to two or more people or situation but the feeling may be different actually.

The English word 'love' has many dissimilar meanings. It can mean affection, benevolent, strong liking, romantic, or sexual implications. The Hebrew word *aheb*, most commonly used in the Old Testament, had a similar range of meanings.

Love in the New Testament

Love in the New Testament does not necessarily wears a different garb from the one in the Old Testament, but it takes a different forms of expression as summarily found in John 3:16. The Love found in the New Testament is the unconditional, unselfish *agape* love. The Greek word for sexual love or romantic love, *eros*, is never used in the New Testament. Even marital love is ideally agape love in its main expression, as in Paul's exhortation in Ephesians 5:25. "Husbands, love your wives, even as Christ also loved the church, and gave Himself for it."

The seeking and bridging activity by God reaches its zenith when God sends his Son into the world to liberate sinners and to provide them with eternal life (John 3:16; Romans 5:7-8; Ephesians 2:1-5). John declares, "This is how we know what love is: Jesus Christ laid down his life for us" (1 John 3:16). God's love is not based on the excellence of the beneficiary (Romans 5:7-8). Because He is love, God does not will for the perdition of His creatures, but wills that everyone repent and live (2 Peter 3:9).

God's Love for Humankind

Love is one of the attributes of God and an essential part of His nature: God is love, and all who live in love live in God, and God lives in them (1 John 4:16).

Our relationship to and with God is like the loving relationship between a child and parent. Like a loving parent, God knows and cares deeply for his creatures: Are not five sparrows sold for two cents? And yet not one of them is forgotten before God. Indeed, the very hairs of your head are all numbered. Do not fear; you are of more value than many sparrows (Luke 12:6-7).

Like children, some people return God's love, and some do not. Nevertheless, He loves all. God's gifts of love and salvation are freely offered to all, even to those who choose the contrary path instead: He causes his sun to rise on the evil and the good, and sends rain on the righteous and the unrighteous. (Matthew 5:45).

The Love of God

Humankind is totally incapable of perfectly or genuinely loving either God or others. Perfect love comes from God who is Love Himself. One must seek God's assistance as a condition that must be fulfiled before one can properly love. The Biblical means of achieving this feat will include: “circumcision of the heart” (Romans 2: 28-29); God's “writing his laws” on our hearts (Hebrews 8:10); being “born again” by the Spirit (John 3:3; 1John 5:1-2).

Hence, no human mind can comprehend the magnitude of God's love to his creatures. We cannot provide a comprehensive account of His love. He “dwells in unapproachable light” (1Tim. 6:16). If God is incomprehensible, so is His love. While we may use human nuances and language to speak about His love, we can never fathom it fully, because it is *divine* love.

It is in this light that the most important commandment as instructed by Jesus is: 'Hear, O Israel, the Lord our God is One Lord, and you must Love the Lord your God with all your heart and with all your soul and with your entire mind and with all your strength.' (Mark 12:28-30). Love of God is demonstrated through or by keeping His commandments and Jesus' commandments (Luke 11:28, John 14:21-24, 2John 1:6), putting our trust in Him (John 14:1), maintaining a humble attitude (Matthew 18:1-4, Luke 18:9-14), and by prayer (Matthew 6:9-13, Luke 18:1-8).

Consequently, when love is not appropriately understood, it is easily misdirected. Its object tends to become the creation rather than the Creator; it loses sight of the eternal for the temporal; it focuses on the self, often to the exclusion of God and others. We become idolaters, focusing a part or all of our love elsewhere. The tendency to become "love breakers" more than "law breakers" becomes high.

The Command to Love your Neighbour

Another important responsibility in life is the love of the other. The second commandment according to Jesus is: 'You shall love your neighbor as yourself.' There is no other commandment greater than these (Mark 12:31).

Love of neighbour is a resolution that we make to treat others with respect and concern, to put the interests and safety of our neighbours on a level with our own if not higher than ours (Although Jesus did not say love your neighbour more than yourself, but it would seem implied). It stresses a practical demonstration in everyday life employing a strong retentive wall to keep people from falling. Our actions illustrate our love. Love for and of neighbour is "love in action", and doing something specific and substantial for others.

The New Testament concept of love closely parallels that of the Old Testament. 1 John 3:18 says: "Dear children, let us not love with words or tongue but with actions and in truth." Believers need to share with those in need, whether that need is for food, water, lodging, clothing, healing, or friendship (Matt. 25:34-40; Romans 12:13). The love demonstrated in the parable of the good Samaritan shows that *agape* love is not emotional love, but a response to someone who is in need. And so, Jesus' command to love others is based on the unconditional love received from God. Since we have been the recipients of love from God and have enjoyed the surpluses of love from others, we must also return love to others that come our way. Since Christ has laid down his life for us, we must be willing to make generous sacrifices or even lay down our lives for others if need be (1 John 3:16).

In a similar vein, when asked to define "neighbour," Jesus cited the parable of the Good Samaritan who crossed traditional boundaries to help a wounded Jew (Luke 10:29-37). A neighbour is anyone who is in need. Jesus also told his disciples that a "neighbour" might even be someone who hates them, curses them, or mistreats them. Yet, they must love even enemies (Luke 6:27-36) as a witness and a testimony.

In the Parable of the Good Samaritan (Luke 10:25-37), Jesus explains that we should consider all the people of the world to be our "neighbours." The Jews and Samaritans were peoples of different races and of rival religions. They had despised each other for hundreds of years and did not even speak to each other. But, in the parable, a Samaritan man stopped to help an injured Jewish man and spent his time and money to give him the best care he possibly could. You too, "Go and do likewise."

You have heard that the Law of Moses says, "Love your neighbor and hate your enemy." But I say, love your enemies! Pray for those who persecute you! In that way, you will be acting as true children of your Father in heaven. For he gives his sunlight to both the evil and the good, and he sends rain on the just and on the unjust, too. If you love only those who love you, what good is that? Even corrupt tax collectors do that much. If you are kind only to your friends, how are you different from anyone else? Even pagans do that. But, you are to be perfect, even as your Father in heaven is perfect (Matthew 5:43-48).

Since humanity struggles to be perfect, all should be wary of the high tendency in humanity to condemn others as beyond redemption. But, humanity has sinned in different ways (Romans 3:23, 1John 1:8). Jesus taught by word and example; no one is to look down or condemn, judge or criticize others (Matthew 7:1-5, Matthew 9:10-13, Luke 18:9-14, John 8:3-11).

This could be part of the reason why the apostle Paul understands Christian love as the greatest and most essential of all the spiritual gifts. "If I speak in the tongues of mortals and of angels, but do not have love, I am a noisy gong or a clanging cymbal. And if I have prophetic powers, and understand all mysteries and all knowledge, and if I have all faith so as to move mountains, but do not have love, I am nothing. If I give away all my possessions, and if I hand over my body so that I may boast, but do not have love, I gain nothing" (1 Corinthians 13:1-3).

Therefore, Love, according to St. Paul is patient, kind, not envious or boastful or arrogant or rude. It does not insist on its own way; it is not irritable or resentful; it does not rejoice in wrongdoing, but rejoices in the truth. It bears all things, believes all things, hopes all things, and endures all things. Love never ends. But, as for prophecies, they will come to an end; as for tongues, they will cease; as for knowledge, it will come to an end... And now faith, hope, and love abide, these three; and the greatest of these is love (1 Corinthians 13:4-8, 13).

Furthermore in another of his letters, Paul said loving our fellowman is the means of keeping other commandments. Let no debt remain outstanding, except the continuing debt to love one another, for he who loves his fellowman has fulfiled the law. The commandments, "Do not commit adultery," "Do not murder," "Do not steal," "Do not covet," and whatever other commandment there may be, are summed up in this one rule: "Love your neighbor as yourself." Love does no harm to its neighbour. Therefore love is the fulfilment of the law (Romans 13:8-10).

It is important to again acknowledge that God is Love and the source of all the love we share. Loving God and loving our neighbour is so interconnected that we cannot have one without the other. We love because God first loved us (John 3:16). Those who say, "I love God," and hate their brothers or sisters, are liars; for those who do not love a brother or sister whom they have seen, cannot love God whom they have not seen, thus, those who love God must love their brothers and sisters also (1 John 4:19-21).

The Concept of Love in Islam

Love encompasses a range of strong and positive emotional and mental states, from the most sublime virtue or good habit, the deepest interpersonal affection and to the simplest pleasure.[162]

The foundation of love for one another is rooted in the nature of God Himself because God is love. This idea of God as love is, however, a dim reflection in the Quran. While the phrase "God is great" (Allahuakbar) is a statement of faith, affirmation and expression in Islam, "God is love" (Allahumuhibba) is not found among the attributes of God in the Qur'an. Islam, therefore, has its profound notion of love, what it stands for, to whom and what it should be directed.

Love in Islam, therefore, is all-encompassing, comprehensive and sublime. The word 'love', *hubb* in its various forms, is

---

[162]"Definition of Love in English".Oxford English Dictionary

used 69 times in the Qur'an. Most of these have to do with human love or love of things and only a limited number referring to God's love. This is in distinct contrast with the Bible, which list 409 uses of *love*. The New Testament alone lists 223. This, however, is simply numbers. There may be other words that are used in Islam to imply love. But, whatever form the word 'love' implies may not necessarily be of any importance so long as there is full submission to the commands of Allah which is the ultimate desire of any Muslim.

The first type of love that Islam professes is the Love of *Allah*. This love makes one to do anything possible to avoid committing sin against *Allah*. This love of *Allah* is to occupy man's heart and conscience in such a way that it overwhelms and conceals everything else. “I never saw a thing but I saw *Allah* before it, after it, and along with it.” The Qur'an says: “The believers are stauncher in (their) love for *Allah*.” - 2:165.

The second type of love is the love of the Holy Prophet Muhammad. This love also makes one to follow the example of the Prophet in all his dealings and manners. To love the prophet is to love God as stated in the Quran 'if you do love *Allah*, Follow me: *Allah* will love you and forgive you your sins: For *Allah* is Oft-Forgiving, Most Merciful.'” Say: “Obey *Allah* and His Messenger: But if they turn back, Allah loves not those who reject Faith” (Qur'an, 3:31-32).

The third type of love is human love. “Human beings can live in blessing and kindness so long as they love each other, show trust-worthiness, and behave according to truth and fairness.”[163] This fraternal love also launches good associations in society when the source for earnestness and affection is of sharing Islam. It means that the Muslim has to

---

[163]imamreza in https://www.imamreza.net/old/eng/. Retrieved 24/07/2018

love his other fellow men regardless of their ethnic, linguistic or cultural background. This includes love of neighbours, colleagues, relatives and even strangers. This type of love persuades the Muslim to help anybody whenever he can. There are numerous *Ahadiths* that exhort Muslims to help anybody who really needs help because it is believed that every of such an altruistic act takes the Muslim one step closer to God.[164]

There are some verses in the Quran that concentrate on the love of the righteous neighbour, especially Jews and Christians: Of the people of Moses there is a section that guide and do justice in the light of truth (Quran 7:159). And We caused Jesus, the son of Mary, to follow in the footsteps of those (earlier prophets), confirming the truth of whatever there still remained of the Torah; and We sent him the Gospel, wherein there was guidance and light, confirming the truth of whatever there still remained of the Torah, and as a guidance and admonition unto the God-conscious (Quran 5:46).

That is why those who have attained to faith (in this divine writ), as well as those who follow the Jewish faith, and the Christians, and the Sabians all who believe in God and the Last Day and do righteous deeds-shall have their reward with their Sustainer; and no fear need they have, and neither shall they grieve (Quran 2:62).

The Quran went on to note that not all of them are alike: Of the People of the Book are a portion that stand (For the right): They rehearse the Signs of God all night long, and they prostrate themselves in adoration. They believe in God and the Last Day; they enjoin what is right, and forbid what is wrong; and they hasten (in emulation) in (all) good works: They are in the ranks of the righteous (Quran 3:113-114). They should therefore be loved as righteous neighbours.

---

[164]Ibid

And there are, certainly, among the People of the Book, those who believe in God, in the revelation to you, and in the revelation to them, bowing in humility to God. They will not sell the Signs of God for a miserable gain! For them is a reward with their Lord, and God is swift in account (Quran 3:199). These category of neighbour should also be loved.

Quran 49:13 summarises it all: O mankind! We created you from a single (pair) of a male and a female, and made you into nations and tribes, that you may know each other (not that you may despise (each other). Verily the most honoured of you in the sight of God is (he who is) the most righteous of you. And God has full knowledge and is well acquainted (with all things).

The fourth type of love is the love between a man and a woman which must be within the charter of marriage because marital love leads the couple to have a peaceful and happy family life. This love is honoured as long as it is within the frame of marriage and this is encouraged in the Qur'an, "And one of His signs is that He created mates for you from yourselves that you may find rest in them, and He puts between you love and compassion; most surely there are signs in this for a people who reflect" (Quran, 30:21). The only love between a man and a woman that achieves fruition is that between a husband and a wife. The love and compassion between a husband and a wife is a gift from *Allah*, and a loving wife finds happiness in obeying her husband.

Apart from the love between couples, there is also the love of the world. This is the platform where a person does not see anything but the world before him. Every thought and action is for some worldly gain. Such a person cannot devote himself/herself to pious deeds for more than a few days. This love of the world also leads to self-love which, if reinforced, becomes more intense, exceeds the limit of expediency, and consequently turns into egoism and selfishness, producing great evil, polluting the person with many vices leading to the violation of the rights of others, and promoting anti-human deeds.

As mentioned previously, *Allahu Muhibba* or "God is love" is not found among the attributes of God in Islam. There is, however, the name *Al-Wadud* or "the Loving One," which is found in Surah 11:90 as well as Surah 85:14. In each case the translator translates "full of loving kindness." This indicates that this quality is imbedded in the nature of God himself and of course would then be infinite. However, Islam is careful in stating that we cannot fully comprehend the nature of God but showing His pleasure and displeasure are part of his nature as creator.

Flowing from the same understanding, the Arabic word *wadud* is related more to the area of friendship and affection. It is applied to one devoted in a relationship and expresses fondness. The word *hubb* carries a much more intense meaning and is used in its other grammatical forms for "beloved," "sweetheart," "courtship," "over," and "mutual affection." It is also elastic, as our use of love in English, where one might express his love for sports, movies, food or other common day interests. However, any attribute when applied to God Himself then takes on an infinite value and meaning.[165] *Wadud* and *hubb* are synonymous; depending on the context one uses each of them. English language may not have the capacity to accurately explain Arabic since they are different languages.

It is important to remember that while the Qur'an tells of the love of God, in most cases it is expressed in a negative fashion, "God loves not ..." or it is based upon human conditions for its

---

[165]FaridMahally "A study of the word "love" in the Qur'an" Hubb Allah fi al-Qur'an in https://www.answering-islam.org/Quran/Themes/love. Retrieved 25/07/2018

exercise. God loves the one who does good, the pure, the just, the trusting, the patient and persevering, the one who takes up arms to fight in God's cause. But where is the room for a God who initiates love in order to win over the lost and erring? Where is He who loved us while we were yet sinners? Where the room is for the one who was rich, yet for our sakes became poor so that we might be made rich? The contrast is too great to overlook. Could we not also reply that, yes, we too love those who do well and are just and demonstrate good qualities. However, that would mean that God only expresses a human love if His love is based on conditions. A revelation of infinite love demands something of the extraordinary, something commensurate with the nature and character of God Himself.[166]

In all these, however, it is not to say God does not love. Quran 49:7 says "But Allah has endeared the faith to you". The word 'endeared' implies affection to his servant. Allah will love you and forgive your sins (Quran 3:31). The bounties that Allah has shown upon His servants are so enormous and uncountable that one needs to show Allah love more than anyone or anything. One's love of God ought to be more than His love to one because as one's creator, he decided to make one a human being and not an animal.

---

[166] Ibid

CHAPTER FIVE
THE CONCEPT OF PEACE

"

The point is, being a Christian does not mean hating or belittling the non-Christians. Being a Muslim does not mean hating or belittling the non-Muslims. Being an Atheist does not mean hating or belittling the religious people. In a civilized society, diversity in religious orientation should be the reason for celebration, not the cause for hatred and differentiation."
- Abhijit Naskar

If the Abrahamic religions live in harmony and understanding, the world will be a peaceful home for all. There are arguments on whether or not the presence of religions constitutes harmony or disharmony. And experience has shown that the answer is yes and no! If religion were to be what it should be, peace would not have been in short supply but a daily meal. There have been serious cases of religious violence in different parts of the world. There are cases of individuals and groups fighting and killing in the name of religion. One is left to wonder if fighting for God makes God more God or less God. Does God really want his creatures to shed blood?

In the Holy Books of the Abrahamic religions, there are, however, some indications that seem to give adherents the command to kill or attack others who do not share the same beliefs. There are doubts, according to different schools of thought that such scriptural passages really call for killing and shedding of blood. Scholars on Holy Scriptures advocate for in-depth reading and understanding of every text and not taking scriptural verses literally or in isolation. In other words, *the sitz im leben* should be the concern of every scriptural interpretation.

It must be said that each religion has the capacity for violence and a capacity for peace, and going through the chapters of history, neither is totally free from peaceful or violent moments. Each of these religions, in their Holy Books contains some teachings or commands on peace and violence. In both religions, God is identified with goodness, mercy and compassion.

In this chapter, we shall see how important religious peace is. True religion loves peace and not the opposite. We shall also see how some of the verses in the Holy Books have been misquoted and probably misinterpreted. If these interpretations by adherents of these religions are not to favour peaceful coexistence, then, could the human interpreters be ignored and the founders of these religions are points of call?

Peace in Judaism

The word peace in Hebrew is '*Shalom*,' and it means 'completeness' and 'perfection'. The Hebrew root word for "complete" or "whole" suggests that according to Judaism and the teachings of the Torah, there is a true state of "wholeness" meaning that everything is "complete."

So, when there is peace in Jewish terms that means things are perfect, things are tranquil, there is adequate security, and a general feeling of physical and spiritual wholeness.

As stated in Ecclesiastes 3:8 peace also denotes the opposite of war, as in "a time for war, and a time for peace" for the absence of war, too, suggests a methodical, tranquil and a flourishing state of activities in a given state of affairs or place. In some scriptural passages the word peace denotes a value, and is used in the sense of fairness, or loyalty (Zachariah 8:16; Malachi 2:6).

Going through the rabbinic texts, one understands that *shalom* primarily signifies a value, an ethical category, it denotes the overcoming of strife, quarrel, and social tension, the prevention of enmity and war. It is still, to be sure, depicted as a blessing, a manifestation of divine grace, but in a great many sayings, it appears in a normative context: The pursuit of peace is the obligation of the individual and the goal of various social regulations and structures.[167]

The concept of peace is generally perceived and understood as concerned with family or communal life, that is, socio-economic and political peace. However, there was some restlessness among the Jews too. Each of the Abrahamic religions witnessed unrest in one way or the other. Judaism may be experiencing peace now, but that does not mean it never had moment of fighting others. Moses went to war, as the following few quotations will show.

According to the Torah in Numbers 31, the Midian War was intended to eliminate the Midianites who had "led the people of Israel to sin against God." Moses commanded his people to fight. He went to war and commanded one thousand males from each of the twelve tribes of Israel to destroy the cities and the warriors of Midian. The "false prophet" Balaam was killed, along with the five Midianite kings. Moses decreed that every male child and non-virginal woman be killed, while the Midianite virgins were taken by the Israelites as part of the spoils of war.

In another instance, Moses said to the people, "Arm some of your men to go to war against the Midianites so that they may

---

[167] *Vardit Ravitsky. "Peace." P.686*

carry out the LORD's vengeance on them. Send into battle a thousand men from each of the tribes of Israel."So twelve thousand men armed for battle, a thousand from each tribe, were supplied from the clans of Israel. Moses sent them into battle, a thousand from each tribe, along with Phine has son of Eleazar, the priest, who took with him articles from the sanctuary and the trumpets for signaling (Numbers 31:3ff).

He (God) has commanded you to completely wipe out the Hittites, the Amorites, the Canaanites, the Perizzites, the Hivites, and the Jebusites (Deuteronomy 20:17). "When the Lord your God delivers (the Canaanites) over to you, you shall conquer them and utterly destroy them. You shall make no covenant with them nor show mercy to them." (Deuteronomy 7:2). These quotations demonstrate that Judaism had its share of violence, and their leading figure, Moses claimed to have been commanded by God to fight.

Having seen the moments Moses went for war, it is, therefore, apt to look at the link between peace and other relevant values, or situations in which different norms might have conflict with each another. For instance, peace as opposed to justice: Rabbi Joshua Ben Korha taught that "where there is strict justice there is no peace, and where there is peace there is no strict justice," and he consequently instructed the judge to "act as an arbiter," that is, to rule for compromise, which is justice tempered with peace.

In contrast with this dichotomous approach, however, we also find another approach that attempts to harmonise the separate values and make them complement one another: "By three things the world is preserved, by justice, by truth, and by peace, and these three are one: if justice has been accomplished, so has truth, and so has peace" (JT Ta'anit 4:2). Here, not only is peace made among men, but also the competing values are reconciled.

Peace is so important a concept in Judaism that Jews have a religious obligation to pursue it. “Seek peace, and pursue it' - seek it in your own place, and pursue it even to another place as well” Leviticus Rabah 9:9

In a similar way, Jews are told that “He who establishes peace between man and his fellow, between husband and wife, between two cities, two nations, two families or two governments...no harm should come to him.” Mekhilta Bahodesh 12. And even that “one may deviate from the truth for the sake of peace...it is permissible to utter a falsehood for the purpose of making peace between a man and his fellow” BT Yevamot 65b and Derekh Erez Zuta.

Peace, according to the Jewish sages, is the ultimate purpose of the whole Torah: “All that is written in the Torah was written for the sake of peace.” Tanhuma Shoftim 18. Peace, in Jewish understanding, is what will save them: “God announced to Jerusalem that they (Israel) will be redeemed only through peace” (Deuteronomy Rabah 5:15”. The Jewish people's desire for peace has been expressed for thousands of years in prayers and in biblical and rabbinic sources.

In the words of the Prophet Isaiah 2:4 and Micah 4:3 that says: and they shall beat their swords into plowshares, and their spears into pruning hooks; nation shall not lift up sword against nation, neither shall they learn war anymore. Also, in the Ethics of the Fathers, Hillel says: “Be among the disciples of Aaron, loving peace and pursuing peace...” (Ethics of the Fathers 1:12). In the Midrash it says “Great is peace since all other blessings are included in it” (VayikrahRabbah 9). The only reason that the Holy One, blessed be He, created the world was so that there would be peace among humankind (Bamidbar Rabbah 12A). In the Amidah, (Daily Standing Prayer of 19 blessings), grant peace, welfare, blessing, grace, loving kindness and mercy unto us and unto all Israel your people.

In Israel's Declaration of Independence, peace was considered a necessity. “We extend our hand to all neighboring states and their people in an offer of peace and good neighborliness, and appeal to them to establish bonds of cooperation ... with the sovereign Jewish people settled in its own land. The State of Israel is prepared to do its share in common effort for the advancement of the entire Middle East.” In the prayer for the State of Israel, peace is paramount. “Please bless the State of Israel...spread over it the shelter of your peace. Grant peace unto the land, lasting joy to its inhabitants. Remove from us all hatred and hostility, jealousy and cruelty. And plant in our hearts love and friendship, peace and companionship.”

The Prophet Isaiah proclaims peace for the Israelites when he prophesied: “Nation shall not lift up sword against nation; neither shall they learn war anymore.” “And they shall beat their swords into ploughshares and their spears into pruning hooks. (Isaiah 2:4). When the Prophet Isaiah wrote these words at the beginning of the seventh century BCE, the ten tribes of the northern kingdom of Israel had been lost, deported by the Assyrian conqueror, and Solomon's Temple in Jerusalem was under threat. Isaiah spoke for a people longing for a universal peace in which nations would live in harmony under a divine system of justice.

Isaiah went on to say: “And the many people shall go and say: 'Come, let us go up to the Mountain of the Lord, to the House of the God of Jacob, that he may instruct us in his ways; and that we may walk in his paths' For the Law shall come from Zion; and the word of the Lord from Jerusalem. Thus he will judge among the nations; and arbitrate for the many peoples.”(Isaiah 2: 3-4). Isaiah 11.4 is another image of peace which demonstrates the Jewish desire for peace: “The wolf shall dwell with the lamb, and the leopard shall lie down with the kid, and the calf and the lion ...together.”

Judaism also recognises that true peace is part of a totality which includes justice and compassion, reflected in the idea of 'Tikkun Olam' - the imperative to 'repair the world'. This concept reflects the Jewish values of Justice (*tzedakah*), Compassion (*chesed*) and Peace (*shalom*), and it has now come to symbolise a quest for social justice, freedom, equality, peace and the restoration of the environment. It is a call to action - to repair the world through social action. It recognises that each act of kindness, no matter how small, helps to build a new world of peace.

On another level, peace was contrasted with truth: It was said in the name of Rabbi Eleazar ben Simeon that "one may deviate from the truth for the sake of peace" (BT Yevamot 65b); in an even stronger formulation, it was said, "All falsehood is forbidden, but it is permissible to utter a falsehood for the purpose of making peace between a man and his fellow" (DerekhErezZuta, loc. cit.).

In all of these instances, even where peace is giving priority and tips the balance, it is viewed as an individual, partial value that must compete with other values.

Notable scriptural passages on peace from the Old Testament among others include:

- The Priestly Blessing (Numbers 6:24-26) ends with: "May God lift up his face onto you and give you peace."
- Leviticus 26: 6: "And I shall place peace upon the land."
- Numbers 25: 12: "Behold I give him my covenant of peace."
- Isaiah 57:19: "Peace, peace to the distant and the close."
- Psalm 34: 15: "Seek peace and pursue it."
- Psalm 119:165: "Great peace to those who love Your Torah."
- Psalm 125:5 and Psalm 128: 6: "Peace upon Israel."

From the above Biblical quotations, it illustrates that Judaism's religious texts overwhelmingly endorse compassion and peace, and the Hebrew Bible contains the well-known commandment to "love thy neighbour as thyself.[168] To love your neighbour as yourself is to live in peace with him. In fact, the love of peace and the pursuit of peace is one of the key principles in Jewish Law. While Jewish tradition permits waging war and killing in certain cases, however, the requirement is that one always seeks a just peace before waging war.[169] According to the 1947 Columbus Platform of Reform Judaism, "Judaism, from the days of the prophets, has proclaimed to mankind the ideal of universal peace, striving for spiritual and physical disarmament of all nations. Judaism rejects violence and relies upon moral education, love and sympathy."[170]

Peace in the Talmud

In the Talmud, Shalom which means peace is one of the underlying principles of the Torah. Proverbs 3:17 has it "Her ways are pleasant ways and all her paths are shalom ('peace')." The Talmud explains that "The entire Torah is for the sake of the ways of shalom" (Talmud, Gittin 59b). Maimonides (a medieval Sephardic Jewish Philosopher who became one of the most prolific and influential Torah scholars of the Middle Ages, in his time, was also a pre-eminent astronomer and physician comments in his Mishneh Torah thusly: "Great is peace, as the whole Torah was given in order to promote peace in the world, as it is stated, 'Her ways are pleasant ways and all her paths are peace" (Maimonides, Mishneh Torah, The Laws of Chanukah 4:14).

---

[168]Firestone, R. (2004), "Judaism on Violence and Reconciliation: An examination of key sources" in Beyond violence: religious sources of social transformation in Judaism, Christianity, and Islam, Fordham Univ Press, 2004, pp 77, 81.

[169]Broyde, M, J. (1998). Fighting the War and the Peace: Battlefield Ethics, Peace Talks, Treaties, and Pacifism in the Jewish Tradition., p. 1.

[170]The Columbus Platform: The Guiding Principles of Reform Judaism, 1937.

Peace is so important that according to Talmudic teaching, the very act of taking someone's life, even when justly doing so, affects, nevertheless the person, as the Talmud regards even a justly court that did order (in ancient times) the death penalty justifiably, that particular court at that time was labeled "killer court" in shame.[171] And even King David, regarded by Jewish tradition as the most pious righteous person, (and his wars were within God's permission or/and orders) was denied building the Jewish Temple, the Talmud explains that when King David) asked "Why can I not build the Bais Hamikdash?" God's answer was: "Your hands have spilled blood (in all your many wars)."

Peace in Christianity

The word "peace" as it is in both Testaments has its roots from the Greek word *eireinei*. It refers to a mental attitude of tranquillity based on a relationship with God in the Christian Way of Life. It is a word which describes the result of a person's proper response to God's Grace. The Hebrew word "shalom" as found in Isaiah 9:6 which Bible translators translate into the English word "peace," has more meanings such as: wholeness, soundness, completeness, rest, fullness, tranquility, prosperity, harmony, lack of worry, the absence of disturbance.

The word 'peace' occurs severally in all the NT writings. It appears mostly in Luke, Acts, Romans, and Ephesians. Peace is use intermittently in its classical sense to designate a condition of law and order or the absence of war, as experienced in Mt 10:34; Lk 11:21; 14:32; Acts 12:20; 24:2; Rv 6:4). It could also be used when referring to the experience of salvation that comes from God or the harmonious relationships between persons.

---

[171]El Talmud by Iser Guinzburg, Editorial MAXTOR, 2009 Pg. 54.

Jesus is known and addressed as the Prince of Peace. This is because of a Messianic prophecy made by the Jewish Prophet Isaiah over 600 years before the birth of Jesus. The prophecy is found in the Book of Isaiah 9, in the Old Testament (Jewish Holy Bible). The prophecy reads: "For unto us a child is born, unto us a son is given: and the government shall be upon his shoulder: and his name shall be called Wonderful Counselor, The Mighty God, the Everlasting Father, The Prince of Peace." Christians believe that Isaiah's prophecy undoubtedly referred to Jesus and pointed to him as the long expected Messiah.

In the Gospel of Luke and in the Acts of the Apostles, Jesus is presented as the one who brings "peace on earth," and one who invites and leads others "into the way of peace" (1:79). Peace is used as a term for salvation; as Jesus said to the woman, "Your faith has saved you; go in peace." (Lk.7:50) and in Lk 8:48, he said,"Daughter, your faith has healed you. Go in peace."

Jesus instructed his disciples to have peace and be at peace with everybody. They are to form a community of peace (Mk 9:50) and to seek reconciliation among themselves before worship when the communal peace has been disturbed (Mt 5:23–26; 18:15–20). The mission of the Apostles was a mission of peace. Peace was offered to everyone; those who rejected peace are left for God's judgment (Mt 10:13; cf. Acts 10:36).

Given the importance of peace in Jesus' ministry, he gave his Apostles peace when he was about to leave them. "Peace I leave with you; my peace I give you. I do not give to you as the world gives. Do not let your hearts be troubled and do not be afraid." (Jn 14:27; 16:33). The risen Christ greeted his disciples with "Peace be with you." (John. 20: 19, 21, 26).

Christianity, in all its preaching about peace and peaceful coexistence, even with the 'love your neighbour' and the 'turn the other cheek' exhortations, cannot be exempt from having dots and references to violence. How can one explain to a non-Christian, the words of Jesus where he said: "But now if you have a purse, take it, and also a bag; and if you don't have a sword, sell your cloak and buy one. It is written: 'And he was numbered with the transgressors and I tell you that this must be fulfilled in me. Yes, what is written about me is reaching its fulfillment."The disciples said, "See, Lord, here are two swords.""That's enough!" he replied.

Having an idea of what took place in the garden of Gethsemane could further illustrate this episode of the sword. Peter draws a sword at Jesus' arrest in the Garden of Gethsemane and slashes the ear of Malchus, one of the servants of the Priest. Jesus rebukes him saying: "Put back thy sword into his place: for all they that take the sword shall perish with the sword" (Matthew 26:52).

Jamieson, Faussser and Brown, in their 1871 biblical commentary, state "...And He said to them, it is enough, not 'Two swords will suffice,' but 'Enough of this for the present'. The warning had been given, and preparation for coming dangers hinted at; but as His meaning had not been apprehended in the comprehensive sense in which it was meant, He wished to leave the subject."[172] Even with this commentary, it is probably not enough reason to be convinced.

In Matthew 10:34 Jesus says: "Think not that I am come to bring peace on earth: I came not to bring peace, but a sword." It is difficult to convince someone that this statement does not

---

[172]Jamieson, R., .Faussett, A.R and Brown , D. (1976). A Commentary, Critical, Experimental, and Practical on the Old and New Testaments Volume 3, Part One. William B. Erdsmans Publishing Company, Grand Rapids Michigan, reprinted, p.329

speak of violence, because sword is associated with violence. Getting the actual meaning of this statement through the use of contextualisation and exegesis will depend on who is the exegist and carrying out the contextualisation.

The historical pages of Christianity show that there were early religious sects that suffered persecutions from Emperors. There is, however, no record of indiscriminate violence or attempts to use terror as a religious weapon by early Christian groups[173] during the Middle Ages Christian anti-Semitism increased and both the Reformation and Counter-Reformation led to an increase in interdenominational violence.[174] This violence was carried out by the adherence of same religion, and it was motivated by selfish reasons.

There are cases where terrorists call themselves Christians, yet they may not be motivated by any particular interpretation of Christian beliefs. For example Andres Behring Breivik[175], who considers himself a 'culturally Christian', claims to have no strong religious beliefs, but he cited saving Christian Europe as the motive for his attacks.[176] He identified with Christianity but never a practicing Christian.

There are historical references where Christians either identified with the 'use of the sword' or abandoned 'turning the other cheek' or 'loving your neighbour'. The Crusades of 1095 – 1492, the Spanish Inquisition of November 1, 1478, the suppression of the Mithraism in the fourth century are all

---

[173] *Ehrman, B. D. (2005). Lost Christianities: The Battles for Scripture and the Faiths We Never Knew. Oxford University Press.*

[174] *Ehrman, Bart D. (2005). Lost Christianities: The Battles for Scripture and the Faiths We Never Knew. Oxford University Press.*

[175] Anders Behring Breivik, since 2017 legally Fjotolf Hansen and also known by his pseudonym Andrew Berwick, is a Norwegian far-right terrorist who committed the 2011 Norway attacks. On 22 July 2011, he killed eight people by detonating a van bomb amid Regjeringskvartalet in Oslo, then shot dead 69 participants of a Workers' Youth League

[176] Ibid

references made to either the abandonment of peace preached by Jesus or the so called interpretation of 'buy yourself a sword'.

In fact, it is difficult to convince one who has chosen not to be convinced and it is simple to convince one who has chosen to be convinced. In other words, for the one who has faith, no explanation needed, and for the one who is faithless, no amount of explanation is enough (paraphrasing Aquinas).

Peace in Islam

The first verse of the Quran breathes the spirit of peace. It reads: "In the name of God, the Most Merciful, and the Most Compassionate" (The Qur'an- Surah Al-Fatihah). This verse is repeated in the Quran at least 114 times. It shows the great importance Islam attaches to such values as mercy and compassion. One of God's names, according to the Quran, is As-Salaam, which means Peace.

The Quran calls its way "... The ways of peace ..." (Quran: 5:16). It describes reconciliation as the best policy (4:128), and states that God abhors any disturbance of peace (2:205). The ideal society, according to the Quran is Dar As-Salaam, that is, the house of peace (Quran: 10:25).

According to Islam, peace opens doors to all kinds of opportunities which are present in any given situation. It is only in a peaceful situation that planned activities are possible. The Quran says: "...And settlement is best..." (Quran: 4:128). Similarly, Prophet Muhammad has observed: "God grants to gentleness (*Rifq*) what He does not grant to violence (*Unf*)" (Abu Daawood).

In Islam, peace is the rule and war is only an exception. Even in defensive war we have to analyse its result. If the result is doubtful, Muslims should avoid war. Stray acts of aggression are not enough for Muslims to rush into war. They have to assess the whole situation and adopt a policy of avoidance when war is not certain to achieve a positive result because peace is paramount.

Given the prominence of peace in Islam, the Quran says: "O You who believe! Enter absolutely into peace (Islam). Do not follow in the footsteps of Satan. He is an outright enemy to you" (2,208). Islam intrinsically calls for peace and fosters a life in complete truthfulness and honesty before God. Therefore, it is important for an individual to believe in God with his own will without force or coercion, and observe God's commands through personal conscientious contentment.

This is one of the reasons why "There is no compulsion where the religion is concerned." (Holy Quran: 2: 256). As stated in the verse, no one can be compelled to live by Islamic morals. Conveying the existence of God and the morals of the Qur'an to other people is a duty for believers, but they call people to the path of God with kindness and love and are not to force them.[177] It is only God who guides people to the right way. This is related in the following verse: "You cannot guide those you would like to but God guides those He wills. He has best knowledge of the guided" (Holy Quran 28: 56).

It is in respect and honour for peace, the Quran 2: 256 says: "there is no compulsion in religion..." The overwhelming majority of Muslim scholars consider this verse to be a Medinan,[178] when Muslims lived in their period of political ascendance.[179] The meaning of the principle that there is no compulsion in religion was not limited to freedom of individuals to choose their own religion. Islam also provided non-Muslims with considerable economic, cultural, and

---

[177]Mustansir, M. (2008), Understanding the Islamic Scripture, p. 54.

[178]Mapel, D.R. and Nardin, T., eds. (1999), International Society: Diverse Ethical Perspectives, p. 233.

[179]Taha Jabir Alalwani (2003), La 'ikraha fi al-din: 'ichkaliyat al-riddah wa al-murtaddin min sadr al-Islam hatta al-yawm, pp.92-93.

administrative rights.[180] This goes to show that Islam does not discriminate on religious lines.

Bukhari 8:387 would look contradictory to 2:256. However, Islamic Apologists have explained that it should be understood in context. The verse says: "Allah's Messenger said, "I have been ordered to fight the people till they say: 'None has the right to be worshipped but *Allah*.' And if they say so, pray like our prayers, face our *Qibla* and slaughter as we slaughter, then their blood and property will be sacred to us and we will not interfere with them except legally and their reckoning will be with *Allah*."

Islamic scholars differ in opinion concerning who the "people" are referred to here. Firdous (2018) in trying to explain clearly said four opinions are popular concerning 2:256, he went further to say:

> The majority of scholars think that this refers to the Arab polytheists. This hadith has been abrogated by the later rulings concerning *jizyah* and peace agreements. Therefore, the Prophet was ordered to fight all the people but then the laws were revealed that excluded the People of the Book from this ruling. A second response says that there is evidence showing that this ruling does not apply to the Jews and Christians if they agree to pay the *jizyah*. The third response is that it's a general term used for specific group of people. The fourth opinion, which seems to be the strongest according to *Jamaal al-Din M.Zarabozo* states that the meaning of this hadith is not that the people are to be fought and killed until they accept the shahaadah. Rather, the meaning of this hadith is that the people are to be fought until they accept the dominance of the law of Allah and withdraw their

[180] Griffin, D. R. (2005), Deep Religious Pluralism, p.159.Westminster John Knox Press.

> opposition. This could be obtained by fighting them, or accepting Allah's law and paying *jizyah*, or by drawing a peace accord between Muslims and others in which the word of Allah will not be opposed in any way by the non-Muslims.[181]

Islam, in admiration of peace, accords everyone the right to live freely and to choose his beliefs. Anyone who wants to support a church, a synagogue or a mosque must be free to do so. There is always freedom of religion wherever the moral values of the Qur'an prevail. Surat al-Mumtahana, 8 says: "God does not forbid you from being good to those who have not fought you in the religion or driven you from your homes or from being just towards them. God loves those who are just." The Muslim is to be good and peaceful to those who have not fought them or driven them from their homes.

God unambiguously states that the existence of people from different faiths and opinions is something that we have to admit and welcome heartily, because this fosters peace; for this is how He created and predestined humankind in this world: "We have appointed a law and a practice for every one of you. Had God willed, He would have made you a single community, but He wanted to test you regarding what has come to you. So compete with each other in doing good. Every one of you will return to God and He will inform you regarding the things about which you differed" (Surat al-Ma'ida, 48). This is a call for peaceful coexistence between people of different creeds and races.

The values of the Qur'an hold a Muslim responsible for treating all people, whether Muslim or non-Muslim, kindly and justly, protecting the needy and the innocent and

---

[181]Nasmira Firdous. "Hadith # 8: I have been ordered to fight in https://quranacademy.io/blog/hadith-8-i-have-been-ordered-to-fight. Retrieved 30.06.2020

"preventing the dissemination of mischief". Mischief comprises all forms of anarchy and terror that remove security, comfort and peace. "God does not love corruption" (Surat al-Baqara, 205). And when it is said to them: "Make not mischief on the earth," they say: "We are only peacemakers" *(Surah Al-Baqarah 2:11).*

A true Muslim makes effort to understand the teachings of the Quran and the Hadith, not just reciting it and interpreting every verse literally. One who professes Islam, true Islam struggles to be at peace with himself and others. As the Prophet Muhammad said in the Hadith of Tirmidhi and Nasai: "A true believer (mumin) is he from whom people's lives and wealth are safe." Allah intends every Muslim to live peacefully and to make efforts for the peaceful coexistence of others irrespective of creed or ethnic background[182] (Emphasis mine).

One who knows what true Islam is, and is a Muslim, seeks to bring others (not just Muslims) close to him, not to drive them away from him. The Prophet declared, in the Hadith in the Sahih al-Bukhari: "In him, there is no merit who is not familiar with others and with whom others are not familiar".[183]

The Prophet is also quoted as saying Islam is welfare (ad-din an-nasiha). 'All creatures are (members of) the family of God' (al-khalqo ayalullah). Accordingly, a Muslim must behave with all others, fellow creatures of God, in the same way as he behaves with members of his own family. Furthermore, as a hadith report in the Sahih al-Bukhari explains, the Prophet stressed that a Muslim is one who desires for others what he desires for himself.[184] Of course such coexistence can only be achieved in a peaceful environment.

---

[182]Maulana Waris Mazhari . The Importance of Peace in Islam in https://www.newageislam.com/islamic-ideology

[183]Ibid

[184]Ibid

A true and committed Muslim is one from whose tongue and hands mankind is safe. In Islam, the right to life is an absolute value, *Allah* mentioned that: "He who kills a soul unless it be (in legal punishment) for murder or for causing disorder and corruption on the earth will be as if he had killed all humankind, and he who saves a life will be as if he had saved the lives of all humankind" (Quran 5:32). Although the preceding part of this quotation deserves some explanation on whether or not the message was for the Muslims, in any case, one thing is important here, which is that Islam as a religion is meant to be in the world an ideology that facilitates the spreading of peace at every level. We should, therefore, understand the ideology of peace given in Islam and everything should be based upon this ideology so that peace will overrule in the world.

Given the quest for peace in all religions, the Quran and the Sunnah being the two most important fundamental sources of Islam cannot be over relied on when the concept of peace is sough in Islam. It is impossible to understand the Quran without reference to the Hadith, and it is impossible to explain a Hadith without relating it to the Quran. There are many Hadiths on propagating peace and its relevance in Islam. The Hadith on spreading peace says: "O people, spread peace, feed the hungry, and pray at night when people are sleeping and you will enter Paradise in peace" (Sunan Ibn Majah).

Abu Umamah reported the Prophet as saying: "Verily, the best of the people to Allah are those who begin the greeting of peace" (Sunan Abu Dawud 5197). On the authority of Abu Huraira[185] it is reported: The prophet said, "You will not enter Paradise until you believe and you will not believe until you love each other. Shall I show you something that, if you did, you would love each other? Spread peace among yourselves" (Sahih Bukhari).

---

[185]One of the sahabah (companions) of Muhammad and, according to Sunni Islam, the most prolific narrator of hadith

For a few decades now, Islam has been through negative criticism more than any other Abrahamic religion with regards to peaceful coexistence. A lot has been said about peace in all these Semitic religions and each religion, it is admitted, is dotted with pockets of violence and the quest for peace, but at the moment Islam stands out to be the most identified with absence of peace towards non-Muslims. The cause may not be far from what is experienced especially with those who claim to fight and kill in the name of *Allah*. It must be stated unequivocally that Islam may not necessarily be what many people think it is.

There are today those who write about Islam as a peaceful religion with relevant quotations from the Holy Quran. These writers do not seem to get a wider readership and followership like those who propagate fighting and killing in the name of Islam. The fighting and killing is seen on news and other media outlets, and the perpetrators claim to be fighting, defending or propagating Islam. They often time quote the Holy Quran to support and justify their heinous activities. For instance, Al-Baqarah 2: 191 says: "And slay them wherever ye catch them, and turn them out from where they have turned you out; for tumult and oppression are worse than slaughter; but fight them not at the Sacred Mosque, unless they (first) fight you there; but if they fight you, slay them. Such is the reward of those who suppress faith" Some Boko Haram members, Al-Shabab, Al-Qaeda, IS, and other similar terrorist groups use this verse to justify their inhuman acts and fighting in the name of Islam.

Quran (3:151) says: "Soon shall We cast terror into the hearts of the Unbelievers, so that they joined companions with *Allah*, for which He had sent no authority". By unbelievers, this verse refers to polytheists and also 'People of the Book' because they believed in the Trinity that Prophet Muhammad believed to be 'joining companions to Allah'.

Quran (4:74) says: "So let those fight in the cause of *Allah* who sell the life of this world for the Hereafter. And he who fights in the cause of *Allah* and is killed or achieves victory - We will bestow upon him a great reward." This is the theological verse suicide bombers use to justify their actions. When Muslims are killed in battle as they attempt to inflict death and destruction for the cause of *Allah*, they will be rewarded.

Quran (4:89) says: "They but wish that ye should reject Faith, as they do, and thus be on the same footing (as they): But take not friends from their ranks until they flee in the way of Allah (From what is forbidden). But if they turn renegades, seize them and slay them wherever ye find them; and (in any case) take no friends or helpers from their ranks." In other words, Muslims should not befriend non-Muslims, except if they accept Islam.

Quran (4:95) says: "Not equal are those believers remaining (at home) other than the disabled - and the mujahideen, (who strive and fight) in the cause of *Allah* with their wealth and their lives. *Allah* has preferred the mujahideen through their wealth and their lives over those who remain (behind), by degrees. And to both *Allah* has promised the best (reward). But *Allah* has preferred the mujahideen over those who remain (behind) with a great reward." This verse criticizes "peaceful" Muslims who do not join or identify with acts of violence in the name of Islam, letting them know that they are less worthy in *Allah*'s eyes.

A few other similar *suras* that they use say: "They wish you would disbelieve as they disbelieved so you would be alike. So do not take from among them allies until they emigrate for the cause of *Allah*. But if they turn away, then seize them and kill them wherever you find them and take not from among them any ally or helper." (An-Nisaa' 4: 89). Quran (2:244) says: "Then fight in the cause of *Allah*, and know that *Allah* Heareth and knoweth all things."Quran (3:56) says: "As to those who reject faith, I will punish them with terrible agony in this world and in the Hereafter, nor will they have anyone to help."

What we have seen above are a few quotations among many related ones in the Holy Quran that speak about violence. This, however, is meant to assist the reader to understand why some people have casted doubts on the peaceful stand of Islam. Some of these verses are used by some people (who claim to be Muslims) to fight and to kill other people. Some of the terrorist groups even claim the prophet ordered them to fight and kill anyone who does not become Muslim.[186]

In my opinion, this is not enough reason to label Islam as a religion of violence. Traces of violence are found in all the Abrhamic religions. These Quranic quotations are not to be taken literally; there are commentaries on them that one is encouraged to know. Those who use these quotations or verses inappropriately, it would seem are ignorant of the peaceful teachings of Islam or understand these teachings literally.

In understanding quotations from the Quran as in other Abrahamic religions, there is need to remember that two things about interpretation of a scriptural text matter, namely: Nothing is to be taken strictly without considering the preceding verses and those following a certain verse. Also, the time and context of the quotation should be put into perspective. In the case of Islam, one must know the history of Prophet Mohammed and his companions at that particular time when a verse or order was revealed. The differences between the Meccan suras and the Medinan suras should be understood and contextualised.

---

[186] Wood, Graeme (March 2015). "What ISIS Really Wants".The Atlantic. Retrieved 30.06.2020

The issue of *abrogation* (nullification) is also very important when interpreting the Quran. In Islamic legal exegesis, abrogation is a theory developed to resolve seemingly contradictory rulings of Islamic revelation by superseding or cancelling the earlier revelation. For instance, the change in the direction that Muslims should face when praying. Originally Muslims faced Jerusalem, but this was changed to face the Kaaba in Mecca.

Islamic apologists and exegetes have a duty to speak out (Some have) and to be heard about the interpretation of misinterpreted *suras* or teachings in the Quran and the Hadith for the sake of those who give Islam a wrong connotation, especially with regards to peaceful coexistence. There are among Muslims those who do not possess a good understanding of the teachings of Islam (the terrorists groups); there are also some non-Muslims who do not know, and it might be difficult to blame them because of the seeming exoneration of violence that is found in some of the verses in the Quran. And interestingly, some are said to have been the words of the Prophet himself.

Securing peace was a major mission of the Prophet Muhammad. Peace, while in Mecca was fundamental for conveying Allah's message to others and for the persuasion of others to Islam. For thirteen years while in Mecca, the Prophet remained committed to using peaceful means of persuasion despite the stringent objection that he was facing. Despite horrific persecution, he and his followers remained peaceful and steadfast. When the prophet could not further stand the objection, he had to leave for Medina. Islamic history records that he later came back to Mecca with a strong force to impose conversion to Islam against the Polytheists Arabs who had objected his message.

CHAPTER SIX

SELF-DEFENSE

The first right of every human being is the right of self-defense. Without that right, all other rights are meaningless. The right of self-defense is not something the government bestows upon its citizens. It is an inalienable right, older than the Constitution itself. It existed prior to government and prior to the social contract of our Constitution.
- Larry Craig

Self-defense is such a natural instinct that should not be denied a human being. When an insect flies close to one's eye, the eye blinks instinctively. The desire to protect life is inbuilt in each person. The Abrahamic religions all acknowledge self-defense and propose its strictest application. Especially when one is convinced that the aggressor is out to kill; one has a natural right to defend the life giving to him by God.

Given the society we live, it is hard to deny someone the right to self-defense. We are not unaware of cases of kidnapping, banditry, armed robbery and all such relevant societal vices that threaten peace. Should citizens then wait for government to protect them? Should individuals rely on the government that seems not to possess the political will and conviction to protect its citizens? In fact, according to the Abrahamic religions, it would seem inappropriate to wait for government to come to your rescue when you are sure an aggressor has come for your life or property; or to kill the vulnerable and those who cannot defend themselves.

This chapter discusses what self-defense entails. It also examines the point one should defend his life or the lives of others. The possession of weapons by citizens has always been a serious issue in governance. This chapter discusses whether or not citizens should possess weapons for self-defense. The use of lethal force and other relevant issues are also discussed in the chapter.

What is self-defense?

Self-defense is defined as "protecting oneself from injury at the hand of others." Self-defense is not about taking vengeance; it is not about punishing criminals but simply preserving one's own health and life when it is threatened by the actions of others. Being a sensitive issue in contemporary society, there is the need to be guided by what we know and accept to be right. In this case, we would want to know what the Abrahamic religions (Judaism, Christianity and Islam) teach about the subject matter. We want our hearts and minds to be ruled and informed by our Holy books, and not by mere emotions or outrageous religious experiences.

Self-Defense in Judaism

The Torah makes it clear that Man is a product of God. Man is made in the image and likeness of God; he is an extension of God. Given that specialty in man, God forbade the unjust termination of man's life and required the death penalty in cases of murder: Genesis 9:6 states: "Whoso sheddeth man's blood, by man shall his blood be shed: for in the image of God he made man." According to the first Book of the Torah (Genesis), God made man and imbued in him a dignity beyond all other creatures. To unjustly terminate life is, therefore, forbidden. Since humans are made in God's image, their murder, therefore, requires the supreme penalty.

Genesis 9:5-6indicates thusly: "And for your lifeblood I will surely demand an accounting. I will demand an accounting from every animal.And from each human being, too, I will demand an accounting for the life of another human being. Whoever sheds human blood, by humans shall their blood be shed for in the image of Godhas God made mankind." In Judaism, these words are very clear about the demand that would be made on anybody that sheds blood; because life is a precious gift from God and when a man is assaulted, the image of God is affected. Given this important position and coverage, we see how this came about.

The Greatest Law

There is one law in Judaism that stands out clearly; it is the law of *pikuach nefesh* (saving lives). It takes precedence over all others. To fail to protect human life simply because protecting the life might require the protector to use violence or to violate a gun control law would be contrary to *pikuach nefesh*.

In the Decalogue, the sixth command states: "Thou shall not kill". Interpreting this commandment literally would undoubtedly obscure its deeper consents. The commandment, after all, does not say "Thou shall not kill humans or animals," but simply says "Thou shall not kill." Lots of ink has been shed on this issue and the interpretation varies; but it remains apparent that the indices show the commandment refers to non-killing of human beings. Some of the Judeo-Christian pacifists who have interpreted the passage to forbid any killing of humans have participated in the killing of mammals, fish, and birds— either directly as hunters, or indirectly, by eating animals which someone else has killed.[187]

It is possible that someone who would not kill lice (live and let live) also would rather die than take antibiotics, in order not to kill the bacteria in his body. But if a person is willing to take

[187]David B. Kopel . The-Torah-and-Self-defence in http://www.davekopel.com/2A /LawRev/.htm

antibiotics rather than die or to crush a wasp before it stings him, then he is willing to kill under some circumstances. If he eats anything other than wild fruit, his eating causes the death of animals (either because he consumes them, or because the non-animal food he eats is grown on land which destroys animal habitats). Therefore, no one applies "Thou shall not kill" literally.[188] Let us now see how life, which is so much cherished by the creator, should be protected, especially against attacks and aggressors.

Exodus 20:13puts it bluntly that "You shall not murder." The Jews say unequivocally that murder is absolutely wrong. This means that premeditated killing of others, killing out of emotion, sniffing life out of someone are all wrong. The 17th verse of the 24th chapter of Leviticus states that the punishment of taking any life is death. In other words, killing is the reward of killing.

Exodus 21:12-15, Numbers 35:6-34, and Deuteronomy 19:1-13 give further qualifications to the prohibition to kill. Here the law deals with accidental killing where there is no negligence. God defines accidental killing this way in Deut. 19:4: "...whoever kills his neighbour unintentionally, not having hated him in time past...as when a man goes to the woods with his neighbour to cut timber, and his hand swings a stroke with the ax to cut down the tree, and the head slips from the handle and strikes his neighbour so that he dies."

In such a case, God says, if you commit unintentional killing, that is, if you accidently kill someone, and it is not motivated by anger or hatred, and there is no negligence involved, then your life is forfeited. You are guilty of killing and could be put to death by the avenger of blood, but there is a way of escape. If you committed accidental killing, and there was no negligence, you would not be put to death if you fled to one of

[188] Ibid

the designated cities of refuge. (The Cities of Refuge were six Levitical towns in the Kingdom of Israel and the Kingdom of Judah in which the perpetrators of accidental manslaughter could claim the right of asylum. ... Outside of these cities, blood vengeance against such perpetrators was allowed by law). Having seen how life should be honoured and revered, let us know examine through the Jewish scriptures, the Talmud and what other Jewish scholars have said about self-defense.

Self-Defense

A Jewish Maxim says:

> "Kill him who unlawfully attempts to kill thee" And "The act of breaking in is the burglar's death warrant."

We have seen the definition of self-defense and the place of human life in the Jewish law. It suffices to remember that the act of defending oneself is principally for the preservation of one's life when attacked by an aggressor or assailant. Life is a gift from God and must be protected in whatever way possible. But, in what circumstances should one defend his life or the life of others?

Exodus 22:2-3 states that: "If a thief is caught breaking in at night and is struck a fatal blow, the defender is not guilty of bloodshed; [3] but if it happens after sunrise, the defender is guilty of bloodshed. Verse 2 states that if someone breaks into your home at night, and you kill him, you are not held guilty or charged of murder. In this case, as says the law, it was at night. The verse fails to indicate the intention (theft, rape, murder, kidnapping, etc.) of the invader. In the night or in the dark, you have no way of knowing if someone is coming to kidnap, to rape, or to murder. You are thus blameless if the criminal is killed in that situation. The defendant can righteously defend himself with lethal force to prevent the commission of the crime.

Rashi[189] writes that killing the burglar is lawful only when the burglar is "in the very act of forcing the entry." In such a case, there is no bloodguilt, for the burglar "has been dead from the very beginning of his criminal act." Rashi explains the Torah thus:

> Here the Torah teaches you the rule: "If one comes with the intention of killing you, be quick and kill him." And this burglar actually came with the intention of killing you, for he knew full well that no one can hold himself in check, looking on whilst people are stealing his property before his eyes and doing nothing. He (the thief) therefore obviously came with this purpose in view that in case the owner of the property would resist him, he would kill him.[190]

The great Jewish legal scholar Maimonides (Rabbi Moshe Ben Maimon (1153-1204) (71) takes a more magnanimous view of self-defense than does Rashi. Maimonides agrees with all the earlier scholars that the rationale for killing the burglar is the presumption of danger. Specifically, the rationale is explained as "(the burglar) was thought to enter with an intention to murder someone."[191]

Mendelsohn[192] after summarising up various portions and positions of the *halacha*, wrote among other things, that the taking of human life is justifiable under the following conditions:

---

[189]An acronym for Rabbi Solomon bar Isaac, who lived from 1040 to 1105. He is one our most important biblical literalist commentators.

[190]Exodus in 2 Rashi, supra note 32, at 277

[191]Talmud, Tractate Sanhedrin, folio 72a

[192] Samuel Mendelsohn was a late nineteenth and early twentieth century Jewish rabbi and halachic commentator. He provides a good summary of what the more prestigious commentators like Rashi and Rambam have concluded.

In the execution of condemned criminals by the legal executioners of legitimate government, (that is, not by vigilantes or individual volition).

In the defense of human life, if one attempts the life of another, as in the case of these terrorist attacks, the crime should be prevented, if necessary, by killing the would-be criminal or terrorist. Such actions are not "murders" they are justified "killings." according to the *halacha*.

In defense of chastity, that is, killing to prevent rape, adultery, incest, or sexual abuses done to minors. I would add to protect minors from any and all serious abuses where killing is the only way to protect the child.

And in cases of self-defense, and that not only when one directly attempts another's life, but again also when he discovers a burglar on his premises during the night (Mendelsohn does not elaborate on the day verses night debate but I assume he agrees with Rambam and Rashi here).[193]

Mendelsohn went on to say that the killing must be for the purpose of preventing a crime, rather than revenging a completed crime, and deadly force can be used only when other means, such as "maiming the culprit," would not suffice.

Verse 3 of Exodus 22 says: "if the sun has risen on him", and you kill the intruder, you are guilty of his bloodshed. In the daytime, it is assumed that the intention of the intruder can be discerned. If he is a thief, he may not be killed by the defendant. However, if the intruder is there to commit a different crime assault, murder, kidnapping, rape, etc., different laws/rules would apply. Though the crime of theft is

---

[193]Shlomo Nachman, (2017) When does Jewish halacha permit one to take a life in http://learnemunah.com/questions/self-defense.html

not worthy of death, kidnapping was worthy of death. "Anyone who kidnaps someone is to be put to death, whether the victim has been sold or is still in the kidnapper's possession (Exodus 21:16). "If someone is caught kidnapping a fellow Israelite and treating or selling them as a slave, the kidnapper must die. You must purge the evil from among you." (Deut. 24:7).

Hence, the *Talmud* goes further to empower bystanders to kill if necessary to prevent a murder, the rape of a betrothed woman, or pederasty.[194] Jewish commentators have agreed that a person is required even to hire a rescuer if necessary to save the victim from the "pursuer" (the *rodef*).[195] In the same vein Exodus 21:29-31 puts it clearly that if a man has an ox or bull which is prone to harm people, the owner is held liable if he fails to confine it and it harms or kills others. If it harms someone, the negligent owner is fined. If the ox *kills* someone, the negligent owner is to be put to death. Likewise, "if one sees a wild beast ravaging "(a fellow) or bandits coming to attack him . . . he is obligated to save "the fellow)."[196]

In a similar vein, under the Mosaic Law, the nearest relative of a person who was murdered was obliged to kill the murderer, providing blood restitution for the death of the innocent. But when a nocturnal burglar was killed in the act, there was no wrong-doing. Thus, his relatives had no right of restitution against the home-owner.[197]

There are two passages that support the use of force to defend an innocent person from an aggressor. They are Leviticus 19: 16 and in Deuteronomy 23:23-27. *Leviticus* 19:16, which states, "neither shall thou stand against the blood of thy

---

[194]Vilna Talmud, Tractate Sanhedrin, folio 73a.

[195]Vilna Talmud, Tractate Sanhedrin, folio 73a[3]

[196]Vilna A Talmud, Tractate Sanhedrin, folio 73a[1] (alterations in original)

[197]Mendelsohn, S. (1968).The Criminal Jurisprudence of The Ancient Hebrews 33 (Herman Press

neighbour."[198] Or in other translations, "nor shall you stand idly by when your neighbour's life is at stake"

Similarly, in Deuteronomy 23:23-27, the passage explains that if a man and a betrothed (engaged) woman had illicit sex in the city, it would be presumed that she had consented; because she would have cried out for help had she not consented. But if the sexual act occurred in the country, she would be presumed to have been the victim of a forcible rape, "(f) or he found her in the field, and the betrothed damsel cried . . . there was none to save her" (Deuteronomy 23:23-27). It goes without mentioning that it was the duty of bystanders to notice a woman's cries, and set her free.

The penultimate positive *Mitzvot*,[199] number 247, requires one "(t)o save a person who is being pursued even if it is necessary to kill the pursuer".[200] Having seen what could possibly lead to the killing of an aggressor or a thief, we now see whether or not Judaism permits the possession of weapons.

Possession of Weapons

The Bible does not out rightly condemn the ownership of weapons. This, however, does not necessarily make its possession legal. We shall now see some scriptural passages with regards to the ownership of weapons.

1 Samuel 13:19-22says: "Now there was no blacksmith to be found throughout all the land of Israel, for the Philistines said, lest the Hebrews make swords or spears.... So it came about,

---

[198] See also Proverbs24:11-12: "Rescue those who are being taken away to death; hold back those who are stumbling to the slaughter. If you say, 'Behold, we did not know this,' does not he who weighs the heart perceive it?"

[199] A "commandment." It can also refer to any Jewish religious obligation, or more generally to any good deed. Mitzvot definition at http://www.jewfaq.org/defs/mitzvot.htm. Retrieved 12.06.2020

[200] Moses Maimonides, Mishneh Torah58 (Eliyahu Touger transl., Moznaim Pub. Corp. 1996-97).

on the day of battle, that there was neither sword nor spear found in the hand of any of the people who were with Saul and Jonathan. But they were found with Saul and Jonathan his son.

Psalm 144:1 says: “Praise be to the LORD my Rock, who trains my hands for war, my fingers for battle.”Psalm 18:34says: “He trains my hands for battle; my arms can bend a bow of bronze.” One is left to consult commentaries for deeper exegesis on these two verses from David, the author of the Book of Psalms. What necessitated these statements? Why and how would David claim to have been trained (his hands) by the Lord for war and his fingers for battle? What sort of war or battle could David be referring to? These are questions that beg for answers. We are also aware that David waged wars and was guided by God to victory Cf 1 Chronicles 18.

We also have accounts of David, not a soldier and not a law enforcement officer, but a youth, employing ranged weapons skillfully (with God's help) against bears and lions. Your servant has killed both the lion and the bear; this uncircumcised Philistine will be like one of them, because he has defied the armies of the living God. The LORD who rescued me from the paw of the lion and the paw of the bear will rescue me from the hand of this Philistine.” (1 Samuel 17:36-38).

We are aware that lions and bears are among the fiercest large wild animals. They were common fearful sight in Israel. They are much stronger than a man (see for examples in 1 Kings 13:24 and 2 Kings 2:24). Only the bravest and strongest men were able to kill a lion (Judges 14:5-6; 2 Samuel 23:20). However, David had killed both a lion and a bear; animals that were stronger than him.

In all these victories by David, we are not told what weapon (s) he used to kill the lion and the bear. We are, however, told that he did not use a sword to kill Goliath but a sling and a stone. Could the sling and the stone be considered as lethal weapons? Or simply weapons. Goliath had a sword with him against David. David did not kill Goliath with a sling and stone, but the sword of Goliath. David only struck down Goliath with the sling and the stone. 1 Samuel 17:50-51 “And so, without a sword, David defeated and killed Goliath with a sling and a stone! He ran to him, stood over him, took Goliath's sword out of its sheath, and cut off his head and killed him.”

In Nehemiah 4, the Israelites have been sent back from captivity to rebuild Jerusalem. They were rebuilding their lives with the sanction of the civil ruler, King Artaxerxes. This was not a wartime scenario. It was closer to a racial integration scenario where racists wanted to kill them. They are surrounded by people who hate them and want to kill them.

Nehemiah 4:13 says “Therefore, I stationed some of the people behind the lowest points of the wall at the exposed places, posting them by families, with their swords, spears and bows”. These were not trained soldiers or law enforcement officers. They were merely concerned residents and settlers, citizens, not professional soldiers or law enforcement agents. Note that these families were *armed*, with “their swords, their spears, and their bows.” This was a situation where they were willing to apply lethal force for self-defense.
Swords and daggers killed Ehud, Amasa, and eighty priests. At longer ranges, we know bows and slings killed men like Goliath, King Joram, and King Ahab. Spears killed men like Asahel, Absalom, the Israelite man and the Midianitish woman, and many others. These are handguns, shotguns, and rifles. These are implements of lethal force. These weapons were used for personal defense and civil defense.

In reference to defense, the question still lingers; against what are they defending themselves? Of course, the crime of unlawful, racist murder and hate crimes. They were defending their lives and their homes. Nehemiah 4:14 specifically says, "...fight for your brothers, your sons, your daughters, your wives, and your houses." It, therefore, seems good and right to defend your family, even using lethal force weapons.

The story in Nehemiah 4:17-23 tells how the builders were wary of their security and, therefore, held tight unto their weapons. It reads:

> Those who were building the wall, those who carried materials did their work with one hand and held a weapon in the other, and each of the builders wore his sword at his side as he worked. But the man who sounded the trumpet stayed with me. Then I said to the nobles, the officials and the rest of the people, "The work is extensive and spread out, and we are widely separated from each other along the wall. Wherever you hear the sound of the trumpet, join us there. Our God will fight for us!"So we continued the work with half the men holding spears, from the first light of dawn till the stars came out. At that time I also said to the people, "Have every man and his helper stay inside Jerusalem at night, so they can serve us as guards by night and as workers by day."Neither I nor my brothers nor my men nor the guards with me took off our clothes; each had his weapon, even when he went for water.

These verses are given here to make clear the situation people faced with regards to security. People whose lives are constantly threatened, whose source of livelihood is destroyed by unknown elements and the government that supposed to defend them seem obviously to be looking away, can easily feel the need to protect themselves and their source of livelihood.

In the Book of Esther we have a historical narrative that speaks to us. In this account, the Jews were under threat of racial violence. The civil authority, through King Ahasuerus, grants them legal permission to use lethal force in self-defense: By these letters the king permitted the Jews who were in every city to gather together and protect their lives, to destroy, kill, and annihilate all the forces of any people or province that would assault them, both little children and women, and to plunder their possessions... (Esther 8:11-12).

So, they have permission to protect their lives using ultimate force. They are allowed to kill and annihilate in order to protect their lives. Now, as people under obligation to obey God, not just to stay within the civil laws of Ahasuerus, what do the Jews do with this legal freedom?

Esther 9:1-5 answers this question. The Jews themselves overpowered those who hated them. The Jews gathered together in their cities throughout all the provinces of King Ahasuerus to lay hands on those who sought their harm. And no one could withstand them, because fear of them fell upon all people. Thus, the Jews defeated all their enemies with the stroke of the sword, with slaughter and destruction. Given the legal sanction to defend their lives with lethal force, the Jews do not choose non-violence. Rather, as it says in verse 11, to protect their lives, they use the sword (verse 5). Here is another example of widespread use of weapons in self-defense a non-wartime, non-law enforcement scenario.

Jewish scholars, especially the likes of Philo of Alexandria, Rashi, Maimonides, and Mendelsohn have discussed extensively the issue of self-defense. Some have slightly different lessons about self-defense drawing from Exodus 22:2-3. They have all agreed with the core principle that self-defense is permissible in cases of necessity.

On the breaking of a home by a thief to steal, the Babylonian *Talmud* explains that:

> What is reason for the law of breaking in? Because it is certain that no man is inactive where his property is concerned; therefore this one (the thief) must have reasoned, If I go there, he (the owner) will oppose me and prevent me; but if he does, I will kill him. Hence the Torah decreed "If he come to slay thee, forestall by slaying him."[201]

We know how Abram saved Lot when he procured allies from three tiny kingdoms by the Dead Sea and led the combined forces in pursuit of Lot, and caught up with the captors near the town of Dan, which is near Mount Hermon, in the Golan Heights (Genesis 14:14ff).

We are also familiar with the Biblical story of Moses how he went out, while in Egypt, saw an Egyptian beating a Hebrew, one of his people. When he noticed no one was in sight, he struck down the Egyptian, and hid him in the sand (Exodus 2:11-12). Moses also saved the seven daughters of the priests of Midian (Exodus 2:15-17). As we have seen above, Moses saved the weak. He felt compassion for people who were weaker than him, and he intervened immediately to protect them.

In these two scenes of Abraham and Moses, we are not told what weapons they used. The Bible does not give any detailed description on the type of weapons used by Abraham. For Moses, we are told he struck down the Egyptian, no mention of what he used.

---

[201]Hebrew-English Edition of The Babylonian Talmud: Sanhedrin, 72a (I. Epstein Ed. Soncino Press 1994).

Self-Defense in Christianity

Life is undoubtedly a special gift from God. Everyone has the God given right to defend his life against what constitutes danger to his life especially against the attacks of an unjust aggressor. For this reason, man has the right to utilise whatever means or force that is necessary to protect his life. The life of another person could be taken as ours when it comes to defending it against an unjust aggressor. The head of a family also has the right to defend the lives of his family members. We now examine what the Bible and the Church say about self-defense or the protection of life.

Man: An Image of God

Christianity got and shares a lots of teachings from Judaism, hence the use of Judeo-Christian term in some literatures. The place of life and its sanctity is appreciated by both religions. There may be some little variations in some cases, but some of them are simply skin deep. For instance, there is a little variation on when life starts in the womb or when the fetus is considered a human being. Another variation is on the 'Thou shall not kill' commandment. Therefore, discussing man as 'made in the image and likeness of God' and the 'greatest law' here will be close to repetition. It is, however, necessary to know the import of this special gift to man by God-life.

The Importance of Life

Life is so significant that Jesus in the Sermon on the Mount, recalls the Jewish commandment 'You shall not kill,' and adds to it the proscription against anger, hatred, and vengeance. The command “Thou shalt not kill” did not prohibit hate, which might be the cause of killing. Because one might observe the command by not killing but hating the supposed enemy and wishing some bad thing happens to him. For instance, pouring curses and wishing death to someone who rapes a woman and escaped without being caught. Jesus, therefore, exposed the weakness and sinfulness of such views. He made anger with a brother a sin equal to murder; and also, such offensive statements as "Raca" and "thou fool," subject to the penalties of murder.

So, Jesus is not prohibiting all anger and insult, but only their inappropriate use. There is an anger which is not sinful. For example, anger that arises from a proper zeal for true religion, anger for the glory of God, anger for the interest of Christ; and anger that is kindled against sin, all manners of vices, false doctrine, and false worship. Those who are angry without a just cause are considered to have sinned against the 'thou shalt not kill' commandment and, therefore, are in danger of judgment.

Is it justified that I defend myself?

As a human being and as one who professes Christianity, do you have the right, or are you justified in defending your life and the lives of your family members? Or should you meekly turn the other cheek (Matt. 5:38-40), come what may? A lot of literature has been written on the legitimacy and illegitimacy of defending lives. There are cases of abortion, euthanasia and a host of other bioethical issues that need answers. However, here, we are concerned about self-defense, especially against an unjust aggressor.

The Church's teaching is very comprehensible on this. The Doctors of the Church and the Magisterium have also made it patent that self-defense is justified and it is not only a right, but in some cases, a duty. In the Catechism of the Catholic Church, the guidelines for when exactly self-defense is legitimate are presented. Let's take a look at what it says.

CCC 2261 says: "Scripture specifies the prohibition contained in the fifth commandment: 'Do not slay the innocent and the righteous.' The deliberate murder of an innocent person is gravely contrary to the dignity of the human being, to the golden rule and to the holiness of the Creator. The law forbidding it is universally valid: it obliges each and every one, always and everywhere." 2258 '*Human life is sacred* because from the beginning it involves the creative action of God and it remains forever in a special relationship with the Creator who is its sole end. God alone is the Lord of life from its beginning until its end: no one can under any circumstance claim for himself the right directly to destroy an innocent human being.'[202]

The Catechism of the Catholic Church states that killing a human being is always a grave issue, which should never be taken lightly. But, then, the Catechism goes on to explain that the fundamental principle of morality is love and preservation of one's self (2264). Christ asks his disciples to turn the other cheek, to love their enemies. He did not defend himself and told Peter to leave his sword in its sheath. However, there is legitimate defense of one's life.

CCC 2263 states: "The legitimate defense of persons and societies is not an exception to the prohibition against the murder of the innocent that constitutes intentional killing." The act of self-defense can have a double effect: the preservation of one's own life; and the killing of the aggressor. . . . The one is intended, the other is not." Legitimate defense is a grave duty for the one who is responsible for the lives of others. The defense of the common good requires that an unjust aggressor be rendered unable to cause harm (CCC 2265).

According to No. 2264 of the Catechism of the Catholic Church, Love towards oneself remains a fundamental principle of morality. Therefore it is legitimate to insist on respect for one's own right to life. Someone who defends his

[202]CDF, Instruction Donum vitae, intro. 5.

life is not guilty of murder even if he is forced to deal his aggressor a lethal blow:

> If a man in self-defense uses more than necessary violence, it will be unlawful: whereas if he repels force with moderation, his defense will be lawful. . . . Nor is it necessary for salvation that a man omit the act of moderate self-defense to avoid killing the other man, since one is bound to take more care of one's own life than of another's.

Self-love remains a fundamental principle of morality. Therefore, it is justifiable to insist on respect for one's own right to life, because life itself is a gift from God.

In other words, love of oneself precedes the love of neighbour, because loving of one's neighbour is baseless if you do not first love yourself in a rightly ordered way. After all, Jesus said, "Love your neighbour *as* yourself." The instinct of self-preservation is based on the fact that life is a special good given to us by God. Each human being has an intrinsic and fundamental *right* to live. Therefore, we also have a right to defend ourselves.

Is it justified to Defend Others?

As your life is a special gift from God to you, so are others to themselves. But, where another person is incapable of defending his life and you have the capacity and opportunity to defend him, it is justified. In fact, defending the innocent is not only a right, it is a duty. We have the ability to lay down our own life for a greater good (as Jesus and the martyrs of the Church did), but we never have the right to lay down the lives of others. I can surrender my own life, but I can never surrender your life for you. The Catechism makes this clear (2265):

No 2265 of the CCC postulates that legitimate defense can be not only a right but a grave duty for one who is responsible for the lives of others. The defense of the common good requires that an unjust aggressor be rendered unable to cause harm. For this reason, those who legitimately hold authority also have the right to use arms to repel aggressors against the civil community entrusted to their responsibility.

It is important to note that this right goes beyond civil community to the life of the family and the vulnerable innocents. When an aggressor is presenting a clear danger to the lives of your wife and children or the vulnerable, you have the right and duty to do whatever is necessary to render them harmless even if it means killing them. How could this be done then? We can now examine the probability of using lethal force.

Possession of Weapons

In some instances, the use of weapons is often employed in the Scripture, and it is often portrayed positively. The use of the word sword could be to mean a weapon or the word of God. The Scriptures are a sword (Eph. 6:17; Heb 4:12). A sword comes out of the mouth of Christ (Rev. 1:16, 2:16, and 19:15). "Put back your sword to its sheath" (Matthew 26: 52).

There is scarcity of the use of weapons and even the word in the New Testament. During the ministry of Jesus, he was careful on the use of weapons, physical self defense or the use of lethal force. Jesus encourages his followers to be peaceful, endure persecution and to love even their enemies. This is evident in Luke 6:27-30 where Jesus said: "But I say unto you that hear, Love your enemies, do good to them that hate you, bless them that curse you, pray for them that despitefully use you. To him that smite you on the one cheek offer also the other; and from him that takes away your cloak withhold not thy coat also. Give to everyone that ask you; and of him that takes away your goods ask them not again." The Christian is called upon to love his enemies. Anyone that does wrong to you should be repaid with good. In other words, the Christian is to show love to all and to live in peace with all and sundry.

In a similar spirit, Paul, while writing to the Romans said: "Never take your own revenge, beloved, but leave room for the wrath of God, for it is written, vengeance is Mine, I will repay," (Rom 12:19). Paul made it clear that they should not take revenge. It is not their duty to take revenge but to leave all to God who repays each one according to his deeds.

We saw that the possession of weapons and to use them appropriately for self defense may be licit but it is not required necessarily by scripture. The disciples of Jesus had weapons in the garden of Gethsemane, and Jesus knew they had them but did not allow them to use them even when they had the right to use them. But what happens when we are faced with death by an unjust aggressor as Jesus was?

Christianity and use of Weapons

The Biblical passage of Luke 22:35-39 speaks directly on the buying of weapons. "Then Jesus asked them, "When I sent you without purse, bag or sandals, did you lack anything?""Nothing," they answered. He said to them, "But now if you have a purse, take it, and also a bag; and if you don't have a sword, sell your cloak and buy one. It is written: 'And he was numbered with the transgressors' and I tell you that this must be fulfilled in me. Yes, what is written about me is reaching its fulfillment."The disciples said, "See, Lord, here are two swords.""That's enough!" he replied.

A few verses before the above episode show that Jesus just had communion with his disciples. They are about to go for prayer in the garden. Jesus reminded them that when he sent them without a purse, whether or not they lacked anything. But this was a different time altogether. Jesus told them, but now if you have a purse, take it and also a bag....

There are different commentaries on this passage and all depends on which interpretation one want to take. There are also innumerable questions that beg for answers on how to apply these words of Jesus. In any case, it is clear that something must have motivated Jesus to use such words. Whether the swords were meant to be used or not, they needed a few, and they had two. It is also clear that some of the disciples had some swords with them as they moved along. It seems Jesus did not stop them, but rather encouraged those who do not have to make effort to buy for themselves.

We lack the capacity to explain why Jesus allowed his disciples to have weapons with them. One may not be blamed to think it was probably in anticipation of trouble from other Jewish sects. Because at the time of Jesus' ministry, there were the Pharisees, Sadducees, Zealots and other Jewish sects who claimed that Jesus was anti Jewish traditional form of worship and other Jewish observances.

Perhaps it was a means of defense against mere robbers. Paul in 2 Cor. 11:26 says: I have been constantly on the move. I have been in danger from rivers, in danger from bandits, in danger from my fellow Jews, in danger from Gentiles; in danger in the city, in danger in the country, in danger at sea; and in danger from false believers." A few dangers are mentioned by Paul. The "perils of robbers". In any case, it is clear that the weapons were carried for a certain reason of defense, and Jesus would have consented to it.

We notice that the Apostles were taken to the garden by Jesus shortly before the passion. When they were in the garden of Gethsemane, the soldiers came to arrest Jesus. The passage says: "And when those who were around Him saw what was going to happen, they said, "Lord, shall we strike with the sword?" And a certain one of them struck the slave of the high priest and cut off his right ear. But Jesus answered saying,

"Stop! No more of this." And He touched his ear and healed him. And Jesus said to the chief priests and officers of the temple and elders who had come against Him, "Have you come out with swords and clubs as against a robber?"While I was with you daily in the temple, you did not lay hands on me; but this hour and the power of darkness are yours." Luke 22:49-5; Matthew 26:51-56; John 18:10-11

In these three passages, you get a sense that Jesus is saying, "Though we have a right to employ our swords in defense of this unrighteous arrest, we are intentionally putting aside our lawful right, and I am allowing myself to be taken without resistance." See how this is expressed: "Lord shall we strike with the sword?" "No more of this." "This is your hour, and the power of darkness." "Put up your sword... or do you think that I cannot now pray to My Father... all this was done that the Scriptures...might be fulfilled." "Put your sword into the sheath. Shall I not drink the cup...?" In another place "Put your sword back in its place, for all who draw the sword will die by the sword.

It is obvious that Jesus had the capacity and the weapons to fight back or use the angelic legions to deliver Himself from this unjust arrest (Luke 22: 51; John 18: 11), but He is willingly giving out his life. For Jesus, violence is not the solution to violence as those who are quick to resort to violence will die by violence (Matt 26:52). The Lord hates the one who "loves violence" (Psalm 11:5).

The Appropriate use of Lethal Force

It is plain that the Apostles weapons in the garden of Gethsemane. However, Jesus willingly asked them not to utilise them for self-defense. In some Biblical commentaries, it is said that Jesus stopped them from using the weapons in order to fulfil the scriptures. With regards to weapons, the pertinent question is: Is it justified to possess a weapon as the apostles did and not use it even when an aggressor threatens to kill you?

This question may sound rhetorical but it deserves an answer. The Catechism of the Catholic Church does not give a direct answer. It mentions that lethal force can be justified if one is left with no choice. Killing should be a last resort after every option has been exhausted. The Catechism, citing St. Thomas Aquinas says:

> Someone who defends his life is not guilty of murder even if he is forced to deal his aggressor a lethal blow: If a man in self-defense uses more than necessary violence, it will be unlawful: whereas if he repels force with moderation, his defense will be lawful. . . . Nor is it necessary for salvation that a man omit the act of moderate self-defense to avoid killing the other man, since one is bound to take more care of one's own life than of another's (2264).

St. Thomas, following the quotation in the Catechism is more or less saying, do not shoot someone for stealing your wallet. That is more than necessary violence. But if someone has pulled a knife on you and by all appearances seem ready to use it, then you can respond in kind. Responding to force with similar force is moderation in self-defense.

We probably know about the 'use of force continuum' which is a standard that provides law enforcement officers and civilians with guidelines as to how much force may be used against a resisting subject in a given situation. A certain maxim says: Don't shoot someone unless you have no other choice. If your life or the life of someone else is in *imminent* danger, you have the right to use lethal force. If there is any possibility of anything else working (verbal commands, physical combat, pepper spray and so on), you have an obligation to try that first.

Similarly, Guzman (2014) used the guiding principles laid down by the Church in a summary as follows:

- We have a legitimate right to self-defense based on rightly ordered self-love.
- We have a duty to protect those in our care, such as our families.
- Force should be used in moderation. Force should be met with like force.
- The taking of a human life in self-defense should be a last resort, when all other options have been exhausted.[203]

Given the importance of life, The *Evangelium Vitae* of Pope St. John Paul II, on the apprehension between respect for human life, obedience to the 5th commandment, and self-defense captures the situation appropriately. There are in fact situations in which values proposed by God's Law seem to involve a genuine paradox. This happens for example in the case of legitimate defense, in which the right to protect one's own life and the duty not to harm someone else's life are difficult to reconcile in practice. Certainly, the intrinsic value of life and the duty to love oneself no less than others are the basis of a true right to self-defense.

The demanding commandment of love of neighbour, set forth in the Old Testament and confirmed by Jesus, itself presupposes love of oneself as the basis of comparison: "You shall love your neighbour as yourself " (Mk 12:31). Consequently, no one can renounce the right to self-defense out of lack of love for life or for self. This can only be done in virtue of a heroic love which deepens and transfigures the love of self into a radical self-offering, according to the spirit of the Gospel Beatitudes (cf. Mt 5:38-40). The sublime example of

---

[203] Guzman, S. (2014) The Catholic guide to Self-defence in https://www.catholicgentleman.net/2014/01/the-catholic-guide-to-self-defence/

this self-offering is the Lord Jesus himself. Moreover, "legitimate defense can be not only a right but a grave duty for someone responsible for another's life, the common good of the family or of the State" (CCC 2265).

Self-Defense in Islam

It is very clear that that the Islamic religion, like any other Abrahamic religion, respects life as a gift from *Allah*. Quran 17:33 says: "Do not take life which Allah has made sacred, except for just cause. And if anyone is slain wrongfully, we have given his heir authority (to demand qisas or to forgive): but let him not exceed bounds in the matter of taking life; for he is helped (by the Law). We shall concentrate on whether or not one is allowed to defend his life or the lives of others in Islam.

Self-defense

The Quran does not only allow self-defense but also permits the use of force in self-defense. Quran 22:39 says: "Permission (to fight) is given to those against whom fighting is launched, because they have been wronged. And indeed, *Allah* is competent to give them victory."[204] The idea of self-defense in Islam and the use of force in defending oneself started immediately after the Prophet Muhammad migrated from Mecca to Medina in 622 AD.[205]

Permission to use force in self-defense is therefore predicated on offending Muslims. This position is reinforced in verse 2:190 where it says: 'fight in the way of Allah against those who fight you, and do not transgress. Verily, *Allah* does not like the transgressors.' This verse was revealed one year after the Prophet Muhammad migrated from Mecca to Medina[206] In

---

[204]Ali, A. (2006). The translation of the Qur'an by Muhammad Taqi Usmani, The Meaning of the Noble Quran.

[205] Daryabadi, A.M. (2002), The Glorious Quran: Text, Translation and Commentary at 603.

[206]Asad, M. (1997), The Message of the Quran at 512.

the words of Niaz, 'Fight in the way of *Allah* against those who fight you' has two meanings. First, it allows Muslims to fight those who fight them, a reflection of the permission given in verse 22:39. The phrase 'who fight you' shows that Muslims cannot be aggressors.[207] This verse prohibits aggression but allows the use of force in self-defense as an exception. Secondly, it refers only to fighting combatants during actual combat (*qital*). 'And do not transgress' means that the limits set by Allah must not be violated: fight those who fight you or use force in self-defense. Verses 22:39 and 2:190 are the two verses that speak of individual self-defense in the Qur'an, but verse 22:39 is a primary verse on this point.[208] Those who dislodge you should be repelled, because they do not wish you well.

The Quran also allows the use of force for defending other Muslims who are oppressed and are unable to defend themselves. Quran 4:75 says: "what has happened to you that you do not fight in the way of *Allah* and for the oppressed among men, women and children". The use of force is allowed in the defense of those who are persecuted for believing in Islam and are unable to defend themselves. It is not every form of oppression, the reason employing force for the sake of the weak must be to the extent of forcing the Muslims to abandon their habitats, especially in cases of genocide of torture.

While verse 4:75 is principally concerned about the defense of the weak and oppressed Muslims, it does not prohibit extending same protection to all others on humanitarian grounds. Qur'an (5:32) states: 'whoever saves the life of a person is as if he has saved the life of the whole of humankind'.

---

[207] Muhammad, N. (1985) 'The Doctrine of Jihad: An Introduction', 3 J L &Religion 381.

[208] Niaz A. S. (2013). The Use of Force under Islamic Law, European Journal of International Law, Volume 24, Issue 1, Pages 343–365, https://doi.org/10.1093/ejil/cht013

The development of such a rule would be in line with the higher value/message of the Qur'an (2:213), i.e., that humankind is one family and the Qur'an (21:170) is mercy for mankind.

Consequently, Quran 5:32 has always been a verse with serious and varied commentaries. Some scholars allude that this verse was not directed to the Muslims but to the Israelites. Because the complete verse 5:32 says: “Because of this did We ordain unto the children of Israel that if anyone slays a human being-unless it be (in punishment) for murder or for spreading corruption on earth-it shall be as though he had slain all mankind; whereas, if anyone saves a life, it shall be as though he had saved the lives of all mankind. And, indeed, there came unto them our apostles with all evidence of the truth: yet, behold, notwithstanding all this, many of them go on committing all manner of excesses on earth.” This explanation may not be appropriate here but it's an attempt by the author to set the records right.

The defensive rule also gives a Muslim leader the right to use force. On the Jihad theory, the use of force is allowed in self-defense; defending Muslims who are oppressed but unable to defend themselves; using force to prevent a humanitarian catastrophe, and allowing a Muslim ruler to use force against rebellion.[209]

It is important to understand that it was during the gradual development of Islam that the idea of self and community defense came to bear. The Qur'an did not allow the use of force and, instead, favoured patience in the early years of the propagation of Islam, that is, the Meccan period (610–622

---

[209] The defensive theory of Jihad is compatible with the 1945 UN Charter. Art. 2(4) prohibit the use of force, but Art. 42 allows the Security Council to authorize the use of force for maintaining or restoring peace and security. Art. 51 allows the use of force in self-defence as an exception.

AD).[210] When Prophet Muhammad migrated to Medina and founded a Muslim community, jihad was allowed in self-defense, that is, in the Medinan period (622–632 AD). In the last year of the Medinan period (9 years after Higira), all the verses relating to self-defense were repealed by verses 9:5 and 9:29, making jihad a continuous obligation for Muslims of all ages.[211]

Niaz presents the following verses in order to provide clear explanations:

The one who defends himself after having been wronged; there is no blame on such people (42:41).

Blame, in fact, is upon those who wrong people and make mischief on earth unjustly (42:42).

And if one observes patience and forgives, it is, of course, one of the courageous conducts (42:43).

(O Muslims), many among the people of the Book desire to turn you, after your accepting the faith, back into disbelievers – all out of envy on their part, even after the truth has become clear to them. *So, forgive and overlook till Allah brings out His command*(2:109) (emphasis added).[212]

In Medina, a new command (verses 22:39 and 2:190) was revealed and force was thus allowed in self-defense, a command alluded to in verse 2:109. The following two verses are cited in support of this argument: Permission (to fight) is given to those against whom fighting is launched, because they have been wronged' (22:39). Fight in the way of Allah

---

[210]Afsaruddin, (2008). 'War and Violence', in O. Leaman (ed.), The Quran: An Encyclopaedia at 687; M. Bin Ismail Al-Bukhari, Kashful Bari: Kitab Al-Maghazi (Book of Ghazqat) (trans. S. Khan, 2008), at 17

[211] Niaz A. Shah, Op.Cit.

[212]Ibid.

[213] Ibid

against those who fight you, and do not transgress. Verily, Allah does not like the transgressors (2:190).

Self-defense became a necessity given that Islam had it rough in Medina for the first few years. There was need, according to Islamic history to employ jihad in self-defense; and this remained in force for eight years of the Medinan period. The Muslim community consolidated itself during this period, and in 9 AH, two separate commands were revealed regarding polytheists and People of the Book (Jews, Christians, and Sabians). The Qur'an, it is argued, said to fight and kill polytheists, but to spare them if they embraced Islam.[213] Quran 9:5 says:

So, when the sacred months expire, kill the (polytheists) wherever you find them, and catch them and besiege them and sit in ambush for them everywhere. Then, if they repent and establish (prayer) and pay (poor due), leave their way. Surely, Allah is most Forgiving, Very-Merciful. The Quran did not indicate where the polytheists became aggressors or when the offended the Muslim community.

The People of the Book (Jews, Christians, and Sabians) were to be fought and killed, but they could be spared if they agreed to pay *jizya* (protection tax) after being subdued. Verse 9:29 supports this argument:

> Fight those People of the Book who do not believe in Allah, nor in the Last Day, and do not take as unlawful what Allah and His Messenger have declared as unlawful, and do not profess the Faith of Truth; (fight them) until they pay *jizya* with their own hands while they are subdued. It is important to remember that the fight here is in defence of Islam.

The argument of the proponents of the progression group insists that verses 9:5 and 9:29 abrogated verses 22:39 and 2:90, permitting the use of force in self-defense. In this situation, "offensive jihad" thus became an obligation for every Muslim: the rules of jihad progressed from a state of patience (in Mecca) to the use of force in self-defense followed by an obligatory jihad against the polytheists and People of the Book (in Medina). According to Niaz, "If this interpretation is accepted, it would simply mean that verse 9:5 obliges Muslims to forcefully convert polytheists to Islam or kill them, which would amount to a rule for genocide. It would also mean that verse 9:29 obliges Muslims to subjugate the People of the Book." [214] But this is not true.

Earliest classical and modern Qur'anic commentators maintain that this verse (9:29) was revealed concerning the expedition to Tabuk, to face the Byzantine (Roman) Empire's army (Mujahid Ibn Jabr (645-722 AD) who were preparing to attack the Muslims in Madinah. But the Muslims were ready with their expedition to Tabuk. The Prophet Muhammad resolved to take up the Romans owing to their resolved to attack the Muslims; the Muslims quickly took it up to attack them in the light of this command from Allah.

However, the study of verses 9:5 and 9:29 in their historical and Qur'anic contexts suggests that the progression argument is untenable. They argue that verses 9:5 and 9:29 do not repeal verses 22:39 and 2:190. To establish our point, we need to examine verses 9:5 and 9:29 in their Qur'anic and historical contexts. We would also need to find out whether the Qur'an had used the 'kill them (polytheists)' language in other verses and contexts as well. Finally, we need to examine the practices of Prophet Muhammad and his immediate successors to find out how they dealt with the polytheists and the People of the Book after verses 9:5 and 9:29 were revealed.

The Qur'an prohibits the crime of genocide. Several verses of the Qur'an and practices of the Prophet Muhammad indicate

---

[214] Ibid

this as shown in Quran 5:32 which states: Whoever kills a person not in retaliation for a person killed, nor (as a punishment) for spreading disorder on the earth, is as if he has killed the whole of humankind, and whoever saves the life of a person is as if he has saved the life of the whole of humankind.

The use of the word 'person' means that any person, irrespective of religion or race or colour, cannot be killed without reasons set out in verse 5:32. It also means that a person of any background can be saved from destruction and death. The principle of humanitarian intervention can be extended to nations and races of any description. It is important to note that humanitarian intervention to protect Muslims from persecution is mentioned in the Qur'an (4:75) separately. It reinforces the point that the ultimate aim of the Qur'an is to prevent the killing of all innocent people.[215]

---

[215]Ibid

CHAPTER SEVEN

SIMILARITIES OF BELIEFS AND PRACTICES

"

Since many of you do not belong to the Catholic Church and others are non-believers, from the bottom of my heart I give this silent blessing to each and every one of you, respecting the conscience of each one of you but knowing thateach one of you is a child of God.
- Pope Francis

Religion is a serious 'business' that requires adequate attention and mutual respect. Each religion has its organised beliefs and practices, usually used as channels of reaching God or relating with others. Each of the Abrahamic religions has its distinct beliefs, practices and rituals; but they all maintain that through such dimensions, adherents are able to connect to God.

Modes of approaching God differ according to every religion. Spirituality is obviously an individual practice, and has to do with having a sense of peace and purpose. In religious matters, one needs to understand that some people place a lot of importance on their religious beliefs and practices. Therefore, there should be respect for others' beliefs and practices even if you do not agree with what they belief and practice.

There is urgent need to know the practices and beliefs of other Abrahamic religions. When we begin to respect the religious practices and beliefs of others, we also set the pace for religious tolerance. It is important to acknowledge each other even if we do not agree at all times. Learning more about what others believe, and why, could help us respect their decision to believe in those beliefs and practices.

In this chapter we shall see some of the beliefs and practices of each Abrahamic religion.

Diversity towards One God

The coalescing characteristic of the Abrahamic religions is that they unambiguously admit the teaching which upholds the revelation of God through Abraham.[216] All are monotheistic, and conceive God to be a transcendent creator and the source of moral law.[217] Their religious texts feature many of the same figures, histories, and places, although they often present them with different roles, perspectives, and meanings.[218] There are lots of ideas, issues and beliefs that show how the Abrahamic religions complement each other. In their views of the cosmos, they believe God created it and guaranteed man to subdue it. God is understood as eternal, omnipotent, omniscient, omnipresent and the sole designer of the universe. God is further believed to possess and dispense holiness, justice; he is transcendent, personal and perpetually involved in the affairs of his creatures.

The Jews understand God as only One and there is no other. God is absolutely monotheistic; theologically indivisible and an unparalleled Being who is the designer and cause of all that exist. The Jewish religion maintains that God is unfathomable and unknowable towards his creatures and it is only God's

---

[216]Peters, Francis E.; Esposito, John L. (2006.).The children of Abraham: Judaism, Christianity, Islam. Princeton University Press.

[217]"Religion: Three Religions One God". Global Connections of the Middle East.WGBH Educational Foundation. 2002.

[218]*Kunst, J. R.; Thomsen, L. (2014)."Prodigal sons: Dual Abrahamic categorization mediates the detrimental effects of religious fundamentalism on Christian-Muslim relations". The International Journal for the Psychology of Religion.*

revealed characteristic that brought the universe into existence, and interacts with mankind and the world. In Judaism, the one God of Israel is the God of Abraham, Isaac and Jacob, who is the guide of the world.

The Christian religion believes and understands God as the Supreme Being that created the universe, preserves and sustains the world. Christians believe God to be both transcendent and immanent.[219] Around the year 200 AD, Tertullian formulated a version of the doctrine of the Trinity that clearly affirmed the divinity of Jesus and came close to the later definitive form produced by the Ecumenical Council of 381.[220] Non-Trinitarian denominations define the Father, the Son, and the Holy Spirit in a number of ways.[221]

> The nature and attributes of God are theologically discussed in Christianity because of their centrality in the faith. This was a serious concern and was discussed since the earliest days of the Christian faith, with the writings of Irenaeus in the 2nd century: "His greatness lacks nothing, but contains all things."[222] In the 8th century, John of Damascus, a Christian Monk and Priest listed eighteen attributes which remain widely accepted universally.[223] As time passed, many theologians developed systematic lists of these attributes; some of them based on statements in the Bible, for instance, the Lord's Prayer, which states that the Father is in Heaven, others based on theological reasoning.[224]

In Islamic theology, God (*Allah*) is the all-powerful and all-knowing, creator, sustainer, ordainer and judge of everything

---

[219]Leith, J. H. (1992). .Basic Christian Doctrine.

[220]Prestige G.L. (1963). Fathers and Heretics SPCK:, p. 29

[221]McGrath, A. E. (2011). Theology: The Basics

[222]Osborn, E. F. (2001). Irenaeus of Lyons.

[223]Global Dictionary of Theology by William A. Dyrness, Veli-Matti Kärkkäinen, Juan F. Martinez and Simon Chan 10 October 2008.

in existence.[225] Islam emphasises that God is strictly singular (tawḥīd) unique (*wāḥid*) and inherently One (*aḥad*), all-merciful and omnipotent.[226] According to the Quran, "No vision can grasp him, but His grasp is over all vision: He is above all comprehension, yet is acquainted with all things" (Quran 6: 103). God, as referenced in the Quran, is the only God (Quran 29:46). Islamic tradition also describes the 99 names of God. These 99 names describe the attributes of God.

The Islamic belief in God, in some aspects is different from Christianity in that God has no offspring. This belief is summed up in chapter 112 of the Quran titled Al-Ikhlas, which states: "Say, he is *Allah* (who is) one, *Allah* is the Eternal, the Absolute. He does not beget nor was he begotten. Nor is there to Him any equivalent" (112:1). This is in contradistinction to the Christian teaching of the Trinity. We shall get back on this.

The three Abrahamic religions specifically tell almost the same type of stories about their faith and their beliefs. This suggests a 'copy right' procedure namely: Christianity from Judaism, Islam from Christianity and Judaism. Judaism with its basis on the Hebrew scriptures of ancient Israel narrates the story of the one God, who created man in his image and likeness, and his choosing of the Israelites to be His people and Him to be their God. Christianity takes or borrows that story but gives it a dissimilar approach and ending by exemplifying the relations between God and his people in the life of a single human being, Jesus Christ. In the same sequence, Islam reiterates some basic components of the same story, confirming the revelations found in Judaism and Christianity, but drawing the story to another ending, Muhammad.

---

[224]Guthrie. S. C. (1994). Christian Doctrine.

[225]Böwering.G. (1998). God and his Attributes, Encyclopaedia of the Qur'ān Quran.com, Islam: The Straight Path, Oxford University Press, p. 22.

[226]John L. Esposito (1998). Islam: The Straight Path, Oxford University Press, p. 88.

The Abrahamic religions do not only correspond but also compete, converge and diverge. They compete in their commitments, converge in their essential structures, which are more proportionate, and they diverge in the way their beliefs work and rely in One God.

In Judaism the faithful are to avoid participating in, or in any way accepting or consenting to the ways of idolaters. Judaism in its classical statement defined its task as passive avoidance, joined with a willingness to accept the sincere convert. Islam prohibits idolatry by destroying its worshipers. Islam calls for active extermination of idolatry, joined with an assertion that, for the idolater to live, he (idolater) must renounce his error and acknowledge the one true God. Christianity on this matter is a mediocre. Unlike Islam and Judaism, Christianity avoids anything that has to do with idolatry and idol worship or eating food for idols. Christianity and Judaism are committed to campaign of evangelism for conversion of those who do not share same faith with them, especially idolaters. But Christianity would slide over compulsion as history would generously reveal. In order to have a clearer understanding of their points of convergence, we now look at their similarities and relatedness.

Scriptures

The Abrahamic religions rely on a *corpus* (body) of scriptures, which are considered to be the word of God. The scriptures divinely inspired and believed to be the work of spiritual men led by the Spirit of God. They are humanly unquestionable.

The sacred scriptures of Judaism are the *Tanakh,* which is a Hebrew acronym to signify the *Torah* (Law or Teachings), *Nevim* (Prophets) and *Ketuvim* (Writings). These are complemented by and supplemented with various (originally oral) traditions: *Midrash*, the *Mishnah,* the *Talmud* and collected rabbinical writings. The *Tanakh* (or Hebrew Bible) was composed between 1,400 BCE and 400 BCE by Jewish prophets, kings, and priests.

The whole of the Torah is considered holy: transcribing is done with conscientious care. An error in a single letter, ornamentation or symbol of the more than 300,000 stylized letters that make up the Hebrew Torah text renders a Torah scroll unfit for use; hence the skills of a Torah scribe are specialist skills, and a scroll takes considerable time to write and check.

The sacred scriptures used by most Christians are the Old and the New Testaments. The Latin Bibles originally contained 73 books. However, 7 books, called the Apocrypha or Deuterocanonical books (depending on one's opinion of them), were removed by Martin Luther due to, according to him, lack of original Hebrew sources.

The first four books of the New Testament known as the 'Gospels' comprise the account of the life and teachings of Jesus Christ. The other books and writings in the New Testament as the Epistles and the Book of Revelation are considered to be divinely inspired.

The Christian faiths especially of Catholicism, Orthodox Christianity, and most forms of Protestantism recognise that the Gospels were passed on by oral tradition, and were not set to paper until decades after the resurrection of Jesus Christ and that the extant versions are copies of those originals. The version of the Bible considered to be most valid (in the sense of best conveying the true meaning of the word of God) are varied considerably: the Greek Septuagint, the SyriacPeshitta, the Latin Vulgate, the English King James Version and the Russian Synodal Bible have been authoritative to different communities at different times.[227]

The Sacred scriptures of the Christian community are complemented by a large body of writings by individual

[227]https://pemptousia.com/2016/10/an-orthodox-look-at-english-translations-of-the-bible/

Christians and councils of Christian leaders. Some Christian churches and denominations consider certain additional writings outside the inspired scriptures to be binding. For instance, Catholics and Orthodox Christians hold unto Tradition as well, other Christian groups consider only the Bible to be binding. In other words, Catholics and Orthodox believe their sacred scripture was written within a cultural background and by people who lived and were influenced by certain cultural antecedents of the time. They therefore, believe not only on what is found in the Bible but also in Sacred Tradition of the people. (John 21:25). Other Christian communities or denominations believe in only what is found in the Bible known as *sola scriptura*.

The holiest book of Islam is the Quran, comprising 114 *Suras* known as chapters. However, Muslims also believe in the religious texts of Judaism and Christianity in their original forms. According to the Quran (and mainstream Muslim belief), the verses of the Quran were revealed by God through the Archangel Jibril to Muhammad on separate occasions, for over a period of some 23 years, beginning on 22 December 609 CE.[228] These revelations were written down and also memorized by hundreds of companions of Muhammad. These multiple sources were collected into one official copy. After the death of Mohammed, the Quran was copied on several copies and Caliph Uthman provided these copies to different cities of Islamic Empire.[229] There are of course, those who think that the Quran came down directly from heaven.

The Muslim Holy Quran mentions and reveres some of the Jewish Prophets, including Moses, Jesus and a few others. The stories of these prophets as found in the Quran are very similar to those in the Bible and in the Jewish scriptures. However, the detailed precepts of the *Tanakh* and the New

---

[228]*Lambert, Gray (2013).*The Leaders Are Coming!. *WestBow Press. p. 287*

[229]Ekrem B. E. (2017). History of the Compilation of the Quran.

Testament are not adopted outright; they are replaced by the new commandments accepted as revealed directly by God (through Gabriel) to Muhammad and codified in the Quran.[230]

Like the Jews with the Torah, and Christians with the Hebrew Bible, Muslims consider the original Arabic text of the Quran as uncorrupted and holy to the last letter, and any translations are considered to be interpretations of the meaning of the Quran, as only the original Arabic text is considered to be the divine scripture.[231]

The Rabbinic Oral Law as also to the Hebrew Bible, the Quran is complemented by the *Hadith*, which is a set of books by later authors recording the sayings of the prophet Muhammad. The *Hadith* interprets and elaborates Qur'anic precepts. Islamic scholars have categorised each *Hadith* at one of the following levels of authenticity or isnad: genuine (*sahih*), fair (*hasan*) or weak (*da'if*) [232]

By the 9th century, six major *Hadith* collections were accepted as reliable to Sunni Muslims namely:

Sahih al-Bukhari

Sahih Muslim

Sunan ibn Majah

Sunan Abu Dawud

Jami al-Tirmidhi

Sunan an-Nasa'i

---

[230]Abrahamic_religions in https://psychology.wikia.org/wiki

[231]Baker, Mona; Saldanha, Gabriela (2008).Routledge encyclopedia of translation studies.Routledge.p. 227.

[232]Uthmān ibn Abd al-Raḥmān Ibn al-Ṣalāḥ al-Shahrazūrī; Eerik Dickinson (2006).An Introduction to the Science of Hadith: Kitab Ma'rifat Anwa' 'ilm Al-hadith. Garnet & Ithaca Press. p. 5

Shia Muslims, however, refer to other authenticated *Hadiths* instead.[233] They are known collectively as The Four Books.

The *Hadith* and the life story of Muhammad (*sira*) form the (*Sunnah*) an authoritative supplement to the Quran. The legal opinions of Islamic Jurists (*Faqih*)[234] provide another source for the daily practice and interpretation of Islamic tradition.

The Quran has references to the "religion of Abraham" as evident in Suras 2:130,135; 3:95; 6:123,161; 12:38; 16:123; 22:78. In the Quran, this expression refers specifically to Islam; sometimes in contrast to Christianity and Judaism, as in Sura 2:135, for example: "They say: "Become Jews or Christians if ye would be guided (to salvation)." Say thou (O Muslims): "Nay!" (I would rather) the Religion of Abraham the True and he joined not gods with God." In the Quran, Abraham is declared to have been a Muslim (a *hanif*, more accurately a "primodial monotheist", not a Jew or a Christian (Sura 3:67).

Eschatology

Eschatology is a part of theology concerned with the final events of history, or the ultimate destiny of humanity. This concept is commonly referred to as the "end of the world" or "end times".[235] In all the Abrahamic religions, there is a belief in the life after death. That the human body must expire someday and the soul goes back to its creator.

The Jews awaits the coming of the Jewish Messiah. Their concept of Messiah differs from the Christian concept in several significant ways, despite applying the same term to both. The Jewish Messiah is not seen as a "god", but as a

---

[233]Momen, Moojan (1985). An introduction to Shi 'i Islam: the history and doctrines of Twelver Shi 'ism. Yale University Press. pp. 173–4.

[234]The human understanding of the Sharia (believed by Muslims to represent divine law as revealed in the Quran and the Sunnah

[235]Dictionary Definition of Eschatology. Webster's Online Dictionary.

mortal man who by his holiness is worthy of that description. His appearance is not the end of history, rather it signals the coming of the world to come.

In Christianity, there is an expectation of the Second Coming of Jesus, though Full Preterits[236] believe this has already happened. Islam awaits both the second coming of Jesus to affirm what Muhammad brought to mankind and the coming of Mahdi (Sunnis in his first incarnation, Shia as the return of Muhammad al-Mahdi). Islamic tradition describes graphically that Jesus' descent will be in the midst of wars fought by al-Mahdi, which means 'the rightly guided one', known in Islamic eschatology as redeemer of Islam, against al-Masih ad-Dajjal (the antichrist) and his followers.[237] In the Abrahamic religions, therefore, there is an individual who will herald the time of the end or bring about the Kingdom of God on Earth.

The Christian religion and Christians have more diverse and definitive teachings on and about the end times and what constitutes afterlife. Most Christian approaches either include different abodes for the dead (Heaven, Hell, Limbo, Purgatory)) or universal reconciliation because all souls are made in the image of God. A small minority like the Seventh-Day-Adventist, teach annihilationism, the doctrine that those persons who are not reconciled to God simply cease to exist. This is expressed in Luke 13:23-28, Matthew 25: 31-38.

In Islamology, God is said to be "Most Compassionate and Most Merciful" (Quran 1:2, as well as the start of all *suras* but one). However, God is also "Most Just". Islam prescribes a literal Hell for those who disobey God and commit gross sin.

---

[236]Those who believe that the destruction of Jerusalem fulfilled all eschatological or "end times" events, including the resurrection of the dead and Jesus' Second Coming, or Parousia, and the Final Judgment

[237]Sonn (2004) p. 209

But those who obey God and submit to Him will be rewarded in Paradise. While sinners are punished with fire, there are also many other forms of punishments described, depending on the sin committed.

On the life after, a number of verses of the Quran, especially the earlier ones, are dominated by the idea of the Day of Resurrection.[238] The belief in Judgment Day is considered a fundamental tenet of faith by all Muslims, because each individual has a reason for being created and is expected to live well against the day of judgment. Day of Judgment is one of the six articles of faith in Islam. The trials and tribulations associated with it are detailed in both the Quran and the *hadith*. Hence, they were added in the commentaries of the Islamic expositors and scholarly authorities.[239]
In Judaism, there are variations of beliefs about the Day of Judgment for all mankind. Some rabbis hold that there will be such a day following the resurrection of the dead. Others hold that this accounting and judgment happens when one dies; and others hold that the last judgment only applies to the gentiles excluding the Jewish people.[240] Although there are traditions in the Hebrew Bible of an afterlife as seen in Naboth and the Witch of Endor as found in 1 Samuel 28. Judaism focuses on this life and how to lead a holy life to please God, rather than future reward. It is, they believe, when one lives and leads a holy life in the present that he prepares himself for the next life.

Mode of Worship

As there are many religions, so also are many forms of worship. In the creation story as found in Judaism and Christianity, God used six days to create all that is in the world and rested on the seventh day. Among the Jews the Shabbat or

---

[238]Isaac Hasson, Last Judgment, Encyclopaedia of the Qur'an

[239]Last_Judgment#Christianity in https://en.wikipedia.org/wiki.

[240]*"Will there be trial and judgment after the Resurrection?".Askmoses.com.*

Sabbath is the day of worship, as Sunday is to Christians. But in Islam Allah did not rest after creation. He is never tired. According to Quran 55:29, "Every day He is (engaged) in some affairs." Friday (*Jumu'ah*) to the Muslims is only a day for larger congregational prayer. It is a higher forum for social cohesion more than the five (5) daily congregational prayers. Friday for the Muslims is not a day of rest. Chapter 62:10 of the Qur'an states "Then when the *Jumu'at Salat* (prayer) is ended, you may disperse through the land and seek bounty of Allah (by working, etc.). this unambiguously indicates that Friday is not a resting day for Allah or for the Muslims.

Mission for Proselytism

The verb "proselytism" as shown in most dictionaries, indicates any effort to convince a person to denounce one's point of view in favour of another. It is frequently used in religious circles, although its synonym which is "convert" seems to be used more.

In the Church's lexicon, proselytism classically refers to conversion efforts being made in order to win over another person from his present convictions. In this circumstance, the efforts made do not respect the prospective convert's freedom and dignity. The effort may involve extreme pressure schemes; telling lies about the other person's current religion or conviction; comparing the seeming weaknesses of another's religion with only the strengths of one's own; attempting to convert children or the weak and vulnerable in opposition to their parents; and even offering worldly inducements to change one's religious allegiance. This is found in different ways and forms in all the Abrahamic religions.

Given the term Judaism, it suggests that it is a religion of the Jews. Conversion to Judaism may not only mean a conversion to a faith, but would seem a conversion to a race or a people. In some cases, an individual may forgo a formal conversion to

Judaism and adopt some or all beliefs and practices of Judaism, but without a formal conversion to Judaism, many observant Jews will reject a convert's Jewish status. [241]Today, we have a few groups that have adopted Jewish customs and practices in places such as Russia, and the Subbotniks but they are not formally converted to Judaism.[242]

Nonetheless, from the beginning, proselytism was a very difficult concept in Judaism. Judaism eschews efforts to proselytize others. Thus, a *locus classicus* in the Talmud in effect instructs Jews approached by a gentile expressing an interest in conversion to suggest that the prospective convert urgently seek out a psychiatrist. Why, after all, would anyone in his or her right mind join a defeated and persecuted people? Only one who persists despite this effort at discouragement is eligible to pursue the goal of becoming a Jew.[243] The Jews were known as a persecuted people because of the holocaust experience.

Judaism states that non-Jews can achieve righteousness by following the Noahide Laws, a set of moral imperatives that, according to the Talmud, were given by God as a binding set of laws for the "children of Noah" that is, all of humanity.[244] The Noahide law or code could be a distraction to conversion to Judaism. This finds reason in the relationship between Christianity and the Naohide law. According to David Novak a case can be made that Christianity is a prototypical fulfilment of the Noahide law since it not only establishes the obligatory moral framework but even meets the Maimonidean requirement that non-Jews observe the code out of belief that

---

[241]Conversion_to_Judaism in https://en.wikipedia.org/wiki.

[242]*Russian Saturday!".Molokane.org.*

[243]Babylonian Talmud *Yevamot* 47a.

[244]Encyclopedia Talmudit (Hebrew edition, Israel, 5741/1981, entry Ben Noah, introduction

it is a product of divine revelation.[245] Judaism like any other religion welcomes converts, but has had no explicit missionaries since the end of the Second Temple era.

Christianity by its nature and form is a missionary religion. One of its forms of development or expansion is by a 'messenger approach' which could also be understood as evangelism. Christianity started as a sect and spread through the Roman Empire. Of course there are as it were, many reasons that led to its spread, but after 313 AD, the Church spread through evangelism. The leader of the Christian sect commissioned his disciples to spread the gospel to all the nations of the world. The prominent version of the Great Commission is in Matthew 28:16-20, where on a mountain in Galilee Jesus calls on his followers to make disciples of and baptize all nations in the name of the Father and the Son and the Holy Spirit.

Christianity in the name of conversion also had Forced conversions. The Church at some point in history forced people to its faith. Of imminent examples is the conversion of the pagans in 313 after Constantine made Christianity a State religion. Also, Muslims, Jews and Eastern Orthodox during the Crusades were forced to be Christians. Jews were forced to convert to Christianity by the Crusaders in Lorraine, on the Lower Rhine, in Bavaria and Bohemia, in Mainz and in Worms.[246] During the Spanish Inquisition, non-Christians were offered the choice of exile, conversion or death; and of the Aztecs by Herman Cortes. Forced conversions to Protestantism may have occurred as well, notably during the Reformation, especially in England and Ireland. Pope Innocent III pronounced in 1201 that if one agreed to be

---

[245]Mitsvah," in *Christianity in Jewish Terms*, ed. by Tikva Frymer-Kensky, David Novak, Peter Ochs, David Fox Sandmel, and Michael Signer (Boulder, Colorado, and Oxford, 2000),

[246]*Abraham Joshua Heschel, Joachim Neugroschel, Sylvia Heschel (1983). Maimonides: A Biography. Macmillan.*

baptized to avoid torture and intimidation, one nevertheless could be compelled to outwardly observe Christianity.

The Catholic Church today regrets the past when people were forced to become members. It acknowledges it a scandal. The Catholic Church, officially states that forced conversions polluted the Christian religion and offended human dignity, so that past or present offences are regarded as a scandal. According to Pope Paul VI, "It is one of the major tenets of Catholic doctrine that man's response to God in faith must be free: no one, therefore, is to be forced to embrace the Christian faith against his own will."[247] Forced conversions are condemned as sinful by major denominations.

Conversion is also found in Islam. *Dawah*in Islam means an invitation to someone to embrace Islam. It is an important Islamic concept which denotes the preaching of Islam. *Da'wah* literally means "issuing a summons" or "making an invitation". An Islamic missionary could be one who invites people to understand Islam through a dialogical method or other licit methods such as books, media etc.

In Islamic theology, the *Da'wah* is aimed at attracting or inviting people within and outside the Muslim community to understand and appreciate the commandments of God as expressed in the Quran, the Sunnah and the Hadith to teach them about the Prophet Mohammad.

According to Quran 2:256, there is no compulsion in religion. Islam forbids forceful conversion to the faith. There are, like in Christianity, episodes of forced conversions in Islam. Cases affecting thousands of people are reported to have occurred during the Partition of India, the Bangladesh Liberation War, in areas controlled by ISIS, and in Pakistan and other

---

[247] *Pope Paul VI. "Declaration on Religious Freedom"*

countries in Africa and Europe. It is important to remember that the religion may be pure in itself, but the adherents could be the problem of forceful conversion, and this should not be taken to be what the religion teaches except there are laws or legislations from the religion that calls for this.

There were forced conversions in the 12th century under the Almohad dynasty of North Africa and Andalusia, who suppressed the *dhimmi* status of Jews and Christians. They were given the options of conversion, exile, and being killed. As it were, Christians then chose to relocate to the Christian principalities in the north of the peninsula, while Jews decided to stay in order to keep their properties, and many of them feigned conversion to Islam, while continuing their Judaic religious practices in secrecy.[248]

During the Ottoman Empire, there was a strong forced conversion that eventually became institutionalised. This was demonstrated in the practice of devsirme, a human levy in which Christian boys were seized and collected from their families among the Balkans, enslaved, forcefully converted to Islam, and then trained as elite military unit within the Ottoman army or for high-ranking service to the sultan.[249] This was an acceptable practice in the Islamic religion during this period. This system (devsirme-janissary) also in the 14th through the 18th centuries enslaved an estimated 500,000 to one million non–Muslim adolescent males.[250]

---

[248] *Maribel Fierro (2010). "The Almohads (524 668/1130 1269) and the Hafsids (627 932/1229 1526)".In Maribel Fierro.The New Cambridge History of Islam. Volume 2, The Western Islamic World, Eleventh to Eighteenth Centuries. Cambridge University Press.p. 86.*

[249] *Krstić, Tijana (2009). "Conversion".In Ágoston, Gábor; Masters, Bruce Alan.Encyclopedia of the Ottoman Empire. InfoBase Publishing. p. 145–146.*

[250] A. E. Vacalopoulos. (1976). The Greek Nation, 1453–1669, New Brunswick, New Jersey, Rutgers University Press, p. 41

Practices in Judaism

In Judaism, as in other religions, rituals and religious observances are central. In Judaism this is found in their law *halakhah*, which means "the path one walks." It is an expanded structure of divine *mitzvot*, or commandments, combined with rabbinic laws and traditions.

In the Jewish life, a lot of things in the life of the individual are given specific and special attention and explanation with regards to the faith. The aspects of domestic life, social life and even political life are taken care of in the Halakhah. The contents of the Halakhah bring the whole of the Jewish life structure into play.

The individual Jewish believer, in order to maintain a good social and religious life, must understand what his faith requires of him about every aspect of life. This is to help the believer in keeping the laws of his religion. Judaism appreciates some important occasions in the life of the individual which would include festivities, family life and the life of the whole community. Some of the important practices in Judaism would include the three major festivals of the Jewish religious year namely: *Pesach* (Passover) commemorates the biblical Passover and Exodus from Egypt: *Shavuot* (Pentecost, the "Festival of Weeks") commemorates the giving of the Law on Mount Sinai; and *Sukkot* (Tabernacles) commemorates the Sojourn in the Wilderness.

In addition, the Jewish religion recognizes several significant occasions in a person's life. While many times the individual is the focus of the festivities, the family, and in many cases the entire community, participate in the commemoration. These special events are some of the most important practices of Judaism.

Before the destruction of the Temple in Jerusalem 70AD, Jewish priests offered sacrifices two times daily in the Temple; since then, the practice has been replaced, until the Temple is rebuilt, by Jewish men being required to pray three times daily, including the chanting of the Torah, and facing in the direction of Jerusalem's Temple Mount. Other practices include circumcision, dietary laws, Shabbat, Passover, Torah Study, Terfillin, purity and others. Conservative Judaism, Reform Judaism and the Reconstructionists movement all move away, in different degrees, from the strict tradition of the law. The women are not allowed to read from the Torah but to say certain parts of these daily practices.[251]

Christian Practices

Before the first quarter of the 16th Century, Christian worship throughout the world was almost the same, only one Church existed, the Catholic Church. Given the Reformation and the advent of Protestantism, Christian worship took different forms. The Catholic Church maintains its Doctrines which are circumscribed in the Magisterium. All denominations have their ways of worship and practices which would include total dependence on the Scripture, emphasis on the Holy Spirit, clapping of hands Eucharistic adoration, baptism, sacraments, and all other channels of reaching or worshiping God.

Islamic Practices

Islam also has its forms of worship. The Muslims observe Five Pillars of Islam which are their core beliefs and practices:

1. **Profession of Faith (*shahada*):** This is the belief that "There is no god but *Allah*, and Muhammad is his Messenger". For one to become a Muslim, he must recite this phrase with total believe and conviction.

---

[251] Abrahamic_religions in https://en.wikipedia.org/wiki/

2. **Prayer (*salat*): All** Muslims are expected to pray facing Mecca five times a day: at dawn, noon, mid-afternoon, sunset, and after dark. The Prayer includes a recitation of the opening chapter *(sura)* of the Qur'an. Muslims can pray individually at any location or together in a mosque, where a leader, the Imam guides the congregation. Women are welcomed but not obliged to participate.

3. **Alms (*zakah*):** This Islamic Pillar is a religious obligation vested on the wealthy members of the community. It holds that Muslims donate a fixed portion of their income to their members who are in need. This also calls on the wealthier members to donate in cash or items, depending on the value of the item and the period, for the progress of Islam and its adherents.

4. **Fasting (*sawm*):** This is observed during the month of Ramadan, the ninth month of the Islamic calendar, when all healthy adult Muslims are required to abstain from food and drinks. It is believed by Muslims that this is the month the Holy Qur'an was first revealed.

5. **Pilgrimage (*hajj*):** This Pillar calls for every Muslim whose health and finances permit to make a pilgrimage to the holy city of Mecca, Saudi Arabia at least once in lifetime. Those who have the financial capacity could do it every year.

In Islam, before the end of Hajj, (not the one called *Ifrad*) all males have their heads shaved then sheep and other *halal*, animals, such as camels, are slaughtered according to a strictly prescribed ritual to commemorate the moment when, according to Islamic tradition, *Allah* replaced Abraham's son Ismael (contrasted with the Judaeo-Christian tradition that Isaac was the intended sacrifice) with a sheep, thereby preventing human sacrifice. The meat from these animals is then distributed locally to needy Muslims, neighbours and relatives. Finally, the hajji puts off *ihram.*[252]

---

[252]Ibid

Chapter Eight

PARALLELS IN JUDAISM, CHRISTIANITY AND ISLAM

Though all three hold some views of the ancestor Abraham in common, they also interpret texts about him differently. For example, in Gen 12:1-3, God promises Abraham that he will be "a great nation," "a blessing" and that "in him all the families of the earth will be blessed." The Jewish understanding of the passage is that the "blessing" will be accomplished through Abraham's descendants, the Jews. For Christians, Jesus and all who believe in him also are descendants of Abraham. And Islam interprets this passage to mean that God make Abraham an imam, or a leader of humanity, and that the "blessing" comes through Abraham himself – Professor Nagel

The parallels among the Ahrahamic religions are meant to help the reader understand the relationship in religious practices among them. There are similarities and differences among them. Their different and similar approaches to issues relating to worship should point to the fact that they pray directly to a monotheistic God. They all have their Holy Books and belief in the Last Day Judgment. What unites these religions should be the point of call to all of them. What separates them should be a call for understanding and appreciation of their differences. Crossing over to another religion should be a matter of conviction not force.

In this chapter, we shall see when each religion was form or started. We shall see the names each of the religions refers to its Holy Book; we shall see the names of the founders and many other things that unite and set a part the three most prominent Abrahamic religions in the world.

The Abrahamic Triplets

Judaism, Christianity, and Islam are Abrahamic religions, also referred to, in some writings, as Abrahamism. They are monotheistic religions and are a group of Semitic-originated religiouscommunities of faith that claim descent from the practices of the ancient Israelites and the worship of the God of Abraham. The term derives from a figure from the Bible known as Abraham.[253] The three most influential monotheistic religions in world history are *Judaism, Christianity,* and *Islam,* all of which began in the Middle East.

Judaism started during the Bronze Age[254] in the Middle East. The Jews, under God's guidance became a powerful people with kings such as Saul, David, and Solomon. Christianity first emerged as a sect of Judaism. It embraced many Jews and their opinions and practices. Christians believe that Jesus Christ is the Son of God and the "Messiah", ("Christ" and "Anointed One"). Within decades of Jesus' death, Christians started to extricate themselves from their Jewish compatriots. Islam originated from the teachings of the 7th Century Prophet Mohammed. His teachings express the will of *Allah*, the one God of Islam. The followers of the Islamic religion believe that *Allah* also spoke through earlier prophets such as Jesus and Moses before enlightening Mohammed.[255]

The Jews call their holy text the *Tenakh,* which Christians call the "Old Testament." Within the Tenakh are the five books of the *Torah,* that begins with the creation of the world by God's

---

[253] "Philosophy of Religion".Encyclopedia Britannica. 2010. Archived from the original on 21 July 2010. Retrieved 3 August, 2018.

[254] A historical period characterized by the use of bronze, and in some areas proto-writing, and other early features of urban civilization. The Bronze Age is the second principal period of the three-age Stone-Bronze-Iron system, as proposed in modern times by Christian Jürgensen Thomsen, for classifying and studying ancient societies.

[255] Judaism-Christianity-And-Islam in https://www.cliffsnotes.com/study-guides/sociology/religion/ .Retrieved 3 August, 2018.

word in the book called Genesis. The Torah primarily tells the story of the early Hebrews and Yawheh's communications to Moses, which established laws on worship and daily life.

The Holy Book of the Christian religion is known as the Bible. It comprises the Old and New Testaments. The Old Testament contains 39 books according to the Protestants, and the Catholics Bible has 46 books, divided, very broadly, into the Pentateuch (Torah), the historical books, the "wisdom" books and the prophets. The Catholic Church and Eastern Christian churches also hold that certain deuterocanonical books and passages are part of the Old Testament canon. The New Testament contains 27 books divided into the four Canonical gospels, Acts of the Apostles, 21 Epistles or letters and the Book of Revelation.

The Islamic Holy Book is called the Quran. Messages that Prophet Mohammed received from *Allah* are a compendium called the Qur'an. "Qur'an" derives from the Arabic term meaning "recitable." Because the prophet could not write or read, he memorised *Allah*'s words and later relayed them to his students. After Mohammed's death, his followers compiled their written revelations. The Koran sets forth standards of daily behaviour and the Pillars of Islam.[256] There are 114 *Surahs* in the Quran, each divided into verses. The chapters or *surahs* are of unequal length; the shortest chapter (Al-Kawthar) has only three *verses* (ayah) while the longest (Al-Baqara) contains 286 verses. Of the 114 chapters in the Quran, 86 are classified as Maccan, while 28 are Madinan.

The three Abrahamic religions share some common beliefs in the oneness of God, the Prophets, Angels, and Satan. All of them also emphasise moral accountability and responsibility, Judgment Day, eternal reward and punishment.

---

[256]https://www.cliffsnotes.com/study-guides/sociology/.../judaism-christianity-and-islam

According to Esposito,[257] all three faiths emphasise their special covenant with God, for Judaism through Moses, Christianity through Jesus, and Islam through Muhammad. Christianity accepts God's covenant and revelation to the Jews but traditionally has seen itself as superseding Judaism with the coming of Jesus. Thus, Christianity speaks of its new covenant with God and New Testament. So, too, Islam and Muslims recognise Judaism and Christianity: their biblical prophets (among them Adam, Abraham, Moses, and Jesus) and their revelations (the Torah and the New Testament, or Message of Jesus). Muslim respect for all the biblical prophets is reflected in the custom of saying "Peace and blessings be upon him" after naming any of the prophets and in the common usage of the names Ibrahim (Abraham), Musa (Moses), Daoud (David), Sulayman (Solomon), and Issa (Jesus) for Muslims. In addition, Islam makes frequent reference to Jesus and to the Virgin Mary, who is cited more times in the Quran than in the New Testament.[258] Mary is usually called Maryam and is mentioned 70 times in the Quran. The Quran notably calls her the most important woman in history. Mary is mentioned only 19 times in the Christian New Testament, along with a handful of other references to her.

Peace is central to all these Abrahamic religions. This is reflected historically in their use of similar greetings which says "peace be upon you": *shalom aleichem* in Judaism, *pax vobiscum* in Christianity, and *salaam alaikum* in Islam. Often, however, the greeting of peace has been meant primarily for members of one's own faith community.

---

[257]John L. Esposito is University Professor, Professor of Religion & International Affairs and Founding Director of the Center for Muslim-Christian Understanding, Georgetown University. A former President of the Middle East Studies Association and Vice Chair of the Center for the Study of Islam and Democracy, his most recent books include Unholy War: terror in the Name of Islam and What Everyone Needs to Know About Islam.

[258]John L. Esposito.https://www.islamicity.org/4654/how-is-islam-similar-to-christianity-and-judaism/Retrieved 3 August, 2018.

Islam is akin to Judaism in its emphasis on practice rather than belief, and on law rather than dogma. The primary religious discipline in Judaism and Islam has been religious law; for Christianity it has been theology. Historically, in Judaism and Islam the major debates and disagreements have been among scholars of religious law over matters of religious practice, whereas in Christianity the early disputes and cleavages in the community were over theological beliefs: the nature of the Trinity or the relationship of Jesus' human and divine natures.[259]

Both Jews and Christians hold a special status within Islam because of the Muslim belief that God revealed His will through His Prophets, including Abraham, Moses, and Jesus. Quran 3:84 says, "We believe in God, and in what has been revealed to us, and in what has been sent down to Abraham and Ismail and Isaac and Jacob and their offspring, and what has been revealed to Moses and Jesus and to all the prophets of our Lord. We make no distinction between them and we submit to Him and obey."

Islam regards Jews and Christians as children of Abraham and refer to them as "People of the Book," since all three monotheistic faiths descend from the same patriarchate of Abraham. Jews and Christians trace themselves back to Abraham and his wife Sarah; Muslims, to Abraham and his servant Hagar. Muslims believe that God sent his revelation (Torah) first to the Jews through the prophet Moses and then to Christians through the prophet Jesus. They recognise many of the biblical prophets, in particular Moses (Musa) and Jesus (Isa), and those are common Muslim names. Another common Muslim name is Mary (Maryam).

Muslims also believe in the virgin birth of Jesus. However, they believe that over time the original revelations to Moses and Jesus became corrupted. The Old Testament is seen as a

---

[259]Ibid

mixture of God's revelation and human fabrication. The same is true for the New Testament and what Muslims see as Christianity's development of "new" and erroneous doctrines such as that Jesus is the Son of God and that Jesus' death redeemed and atoned for humankind's original sin.[260]

To demonstrate the similarities and differences between the three Abrahamic religions, the following chart shows and compares the origins, beliefs and practices of Judaism, Christianity and Islam. Please note that beliefs and practices are oversimplified for brevity's sake.

Topic	**Christianity**	**Islam**	**Judaism**
Origin of the Name	From the Greek:*christos*, 'Anointed' - referring to Jesus Christ.	Derived from an Arabic word for 'submission'. Also related to the Arabic word *salaam*, 'peace'.	From the Hebrew:*Yehudim*, 'Judah'.
Founder	JesusChrist (c. 4 B.C. - 30 A.D.)	Mohammed (570 - 632 A.D.)[1]	Abraham (First Patriarch, born c. 1800 B.C.)
Divisions	Three main groups: Orthodox, Protestant and Roman Catholic.	Two main groups: Sunni and Shia (The division occurred due to a dispute as to the legitimate successor of the prophet Mohammed). There is also a mystical/ascetic movement in Islam known as Sufi.	Several divisions, including Hasidic, Conservative and Reform Judaism. Ethnic groupings include Ashkenazi (The majority) and Sephardi Jews.
Followers (2009 Estimates)[2]	2,200 Million (2.2 Billion)	1,500 Million (1.5 Billion)	14 Million
Nature of God	One God, who exists in three distinct persons (The Trinity): Father, Son and Holy Spirit (Matthew 28:19).	One God (Arabic: *Allah*), who is not a trinity. The Islamic view of God is called strict Monotheism (Quran 112:1).	One God (known in English as 'Yahweh' or 'Jehovah') - "...Hear Israel, the Lord is our God, the Lord is one." (Deuteronomy 6:4).

[260] John L. Esposito. Ibid

Topic	Christianity	Islam	Judaism
Holy Book(s)	The Bible (from the Greek:*Biblos*, 'books'), given by God to man. The Bible writers were inspired by God in their writings. Thus Christians refer to the Bible as the *Word of God* (2 Timothy 3:16).	The Quran or Koran (Arabic: 'recitation'), revealed to the prophet Mohammed over a period of about 20 years. The Quran is the final revelation given by Allah to mankind.	The Hebrew Tanakh, similar to the Christian Old Testament, comprised of the Torah (Hebrew: 'Law'), Nevi'im ('Prophets') and Ketuvim ('Writings').
Jesus Christ	The second person of the Trinity and born of the Virgin Mary. "...true God from true God" (Nicene Creed)	Isa (Jesus) was a prophet, sent by Allah and born of the Virgin Mary, but not divine (Quran 5:17).	An ordinary Jew, not the *Messiah* nor a divine person.
Jesus Christ, The Mission of	To reconcile Man to God, through his death as a sacrifice for the sins of all mankind.	To proclaim the *Injil*, or gospel. This gospel has been corrupted over time by human additions and alterations.	As Judaism rejects the idea of Jesus as *Messiah*, his mission is of no relevance.
Jesus Christ, The Death of	"...For our sake he was crucified...he suffered death and was buried. On the third day he rose again...he ascended into heaven..." (Nicene Creed)	Jesus was not crucified (Quran 4:157), but was raised to Heaven by Allah (4:158).	Jesus was crucified for his claim to be divine.
Holy Spirit	The third person of the Trinity, truly divine: "....with the Father and the Son he is worshipped and glorified." (Nicene Creed)	Identical with the Angel Gabriel, who appeared to the Prophet Mohammed giving him the Quranic text.	Not a distinct person, but a divine power which for example, was given to the Prophets.
Other Traditions	The writings of the early church fathers and ecumenical councils, including the Creeds.	The Hadith, a collection of traditions/sayings of the Prophet Mohammed. The Hadith functions as a supplement to the Quran, giving guidance to Muslims for daily living.	The Talmud, an oral tradition explaining and interpreting the Tanakh. It includes the Mishnah - a code of Jewish law.

Topic	Christianity	Islam	Judaism
Examples of Rituals	The Sacraments, including Baptism and Holy Communion (Eucharist). In Orthodoxy and Roman Catholicism, five more are added, viz: Confirmation (Chrismation), Marriage, Penance, Holy Orders and Anointing of the sick. Prayer is also an important part of the faith.	Five important rituals (known as the pillars of Islam): 1. Shahadah - A profession of faith. 2. Salat - Prayer five times daily. 3. Zakat - alms giving. 4. Sawm - Fasting during the Holy month of Ramadan. 5. Hajj - Pilgrimage to the Holy city of Mecca.	Rituals include the Circumcision of newly born Jewish males, Barmitzvah - a ceremony marking the 'coming of age' of Jewish Boys and observation of the Sabbath (Shabat). As in the other faiths, prayer is important. The Jewish prayer book is called the siddur.
Sin	We inherit a sinful nature through our common ancestor Adam, who rebelled against God. Jesus Christ atoned for our sins through his death on the Cross (Romans 5:12-17).	There is no concept of original sin, nor vicarious atonement. All Humans are born sinless, but human weakness leads to sin.	Judaism rejects the doctrine of original sin. Atonement for sins committed is made through seeking forgiveness from God in prayer and repentance. In addition, the day of atonement (Yom Kippur) is set aside specially for this purpose.
Salvation	By grace through faith in Jesus Christ (Ephesians 2:8-9).[3]	Achieved through good works, thus personal righteousness must outweigh personal sin (Quran 23:101-103).	Through good works, prayers and the grace of God. There is no parallel to the Christian view of substitutionary atonement.
Hell	A place of everlasting punishment for the unrighteous (Matthew 25:46). There is no crossover between Heaven and Hell.	A place of torment and fire (Quran 25:65, 104:6-7). In Islam, Hell is known as *Jahannam*. Jahannam has several levels and a person may not necessarily spend eternity there.	Traditionally, there is the concept of Gehinnom or Gehenna - those who die in sin may suffer temporary punishment, but certain sins merit eternal punishment. However, Judaism's ideas of the afterlife have varied widely among different groups and in different time periods. For the most part, Judaism does not emphasize the afterlife.

INDEX

W

www.ingramcontent.com/pod-product-compliance
Ingram Content Group UK Ltd.
Pitfield, Milton Keynes, MK11 3LW, UK
UKHW042019190726
13854UKWH00005B/2370